THE CITY AND
THE SIGN

THE CITY AND
THE SIGN

An Interpretation of the Book of Jonah

by

Geoffrey T. Bull

HODDER AND STOUGHTON

'To be alive in such an age! To live to it!
    To give to it!
What if thy soul hath drunk the dregs?
Fling forth thy sorrow to the wind;
Link thy cause with human kind.
The passion of a larger claim will put thy
    puny griefs to shame.'
                              Selected

ACKNOWLEDGEMENTS

The author wishes to express his appreciation to:

The Chicago University Press for permission to use the extract from D. D. Luckenbill's *Ancient Records of Assyria and Babylon* on pp. 109–10.

A Dr Babcock for his poem on pp. 145–6.

A poet named Teichmer for the quotation on p. 156.

The author of the poem on p. 5 whose name could not be ascertained.

The writers and contributors of a variety of Biblical reference works, and especially to George Roux for his work *Ancient Iraq* (George Allen & Unwin, 1963) which provided such helpful information relating to the history and culture of Assyria, the fortunes of the city of Nineveh and the times of Jonah.

All those over the years who have taught him the Holy Scriptures, and whose thoughts are so often interwoven with his own.

CONTENTS

PROLOGUE

'The eyes of the Lord
Are in every place
Keeping watch on the evil,
Keeping watch on the good.'[1]

'There's Some-One looking!' The cry shoots through us and
evokes immediate response. Parade and masquerade, guilt
and endeavour, spring to attention and take up their
stations. We are discovered and all our posture hastens to
adjust. To flout or pander? Which shall it be? Play up?
Play down? But why the question? The veiled discrepancy
of what we are and what we seem is out!

We must admit the eyes of men are strong to govern.
For most, the world is still 'a stage on which we strut and
fret'; and audience-response, the thing we prize above the
truth our lips profess. And are there lodgers in our minds,
the harboured secret and the furtive guilt? Our shifting
eyes will soon betray us. A peering public probes our cur-
tains. It is outrageous! Why do they do it? The answer is
not hard to find. They want our person not our pride.
Mere image will no longer do. We must be real.

Today we are a gadding race. Sight-seeing is our life.
Like vultures eager for their carrion, we feed on every new
sensation. But in the seeing of the sights, we are ourselves,
the sights men see. We would observe, but once observed,
soon turn resentful. Can withered 'fig-leaves' hide our
shame?

Yet there is One, Who seen by none, is every man be-
holding. He is the Author of all sight, beneath Whose high
surveillance, we all must live and have our being. He

[1] Proverbs 15 v. 3.

knows our vain façade but seeks in love our inner-man. Like lamps of fire, His eyes discern us. As eyes of doves, His eyes fix on us. His holy gaze, His tender stare know no escaping, till all the secrets of our lives surrender. With ceaseless scrutiny He scans the earth. All heights and depths His laser-eyes are searching. He sees where no man sees, Who seeking, finds, and finding, saves.

This is the seed of fear, that flowers in wisdom; the only hope of true repentance; the only likelihood of faith. To think and speak, to act and feel, as seen by The Invisible; to let His own reality pervade us, till we perceive, what being real involves. To find Him near upon the Sands of Time and say with thankfulness, 'Thou seest me.' To be like Jesus Christ, Who faced with human heart-break and a stone-sealed tomb, could say, 'I thank Thee, Father, that Thou hearest always . . .'

Be then alerted! Some-One's looking! Some-One's listening!

'His eyes behold, His eyelids try . . .
His ears are open to our cry . . .'

I

JONAH AND THE GREAT MISTAKE

POINT OF FOCUS
A POOL OF SLIME
THE JOPPA DILEMMA
THE CHOSEN VESSEL

THE BOOK OF JONAH

Chapter 1 v. 1–3

Now the word of the LORD came unto Jonah the son the
Amittai, saying,

Arise, go to Nineveh, that great city, and cry against it; for
their wickedness is come up before me.

But Jonah rose up to flee unto Tarshish from the presence of
the LORD, and went down to Joppa; and he found a ship going to
Tarshish: so he paid the fare thereof, and went down into it, to
go with them unto Tarshish from the presence of the LORD.

CHAPTER 1

POINT OF FOCUS

I only turned a page but in that moment, a score and seven
centuries fled . . .

How could it be? Was I transported there, or did these
men and things of far-off days find place in me? Sequence
and consequence, it might be said, are Time's constituents,
yet must Eternity alone provide the answer of our present
riddle? Before the womb, beyond the tomb, our origins
and destinies contain the clues to life's enigma. On all our
shores, our little feet splash in the shallows of The Infinite.
From grains of sand and frosty stars, the frontiers of Time
swing out upon the everlastings of the God who made us;
the God who found a friend in Abraham, and seeks us still.

One gulliver-like step from this our lilliputian earth;
one flight of swiftest fancy, beyond all astronaut achievement and we can find a tiny plot on some unchartered
sphere, where earthly things of long ago are only happen-
ing now. We need, of course, one indispensable proviso,
equipment competent, to capture and interpret, light and
sound already centuries old; but given this, the ancient
maxim blooms with fresh significance: 'That which hath
been is now and that which is to be, it hath already been.'[1]

But must we needs go outward to go backward? Why
not go inward? Is outer space the sole venue for ponder-
ing the past? Is there no inner space locked in the mystery
of our being? Though fallen, bruised and soiled, the
spirits of the men God makes, still last for ever. The
border marches of the realm unseen, lie otherwhere than
through the star-strewn wastes above. The eternal frontiers

[1] Ecclesiastes 3 v. 15.

of the Most High God are scored all through us too. In every man the temporal and the eternal meet. He puts the ages in our hearts. Each newborn babe is made a reservoir, to which the varied streams of history and heredity must flow, and more than that, through which the voice of God to man flows on. Once stirred, a human being finds within, a deep that answers to the distant past. In each succeeding generation, the children long for stories of their parents' youth. There is that 'something way back there' that has to *do* with us and such nostalgia marks us all. Perhaps the thought lies somewhere in the words of Paul: 'Now these things befell them by way of warning . . . they were written to fit us for right action . . . we in whose days, the ages have reached their climax.'

That which men did before us, be it deemed in faith or folly, has, far down the stream of life, been poured into our present generation. In many ways we act today, coloured by trend and trait untraceable. Patterns of prejudice and passion intertwine within each one, until we do and say we know not what. We are the sum of all man's yesterdays and God's eternities. Yet as our forbears were responsible, so we bear still, a God-bestowed responsibility, which things of past and present worlds can never totally annul. As living now, we have one great advantage. We are forewarned, although our trust from God is greater. To use our heritage and gift is then our task. To diagnose and learn the past. To take the greater light and wielding greater faith break forth upon our age, to slay its dread Goliaths, with our slings and stones. To turn men heavenward from hell; and from the deadness of a thousand things, point them to Him, who lives to answer every human need. Here is our destiny, on whom the ends of all the world are come, in whom are all the world's beginnings found.

Perhaps it was not strange, that when I turned the page,

a score and seven centuries fled and there I found myself amidst the hot and breathless streets of old Gath-Hepher ...

The sand beneath my feet burned like a furnace. The whitewashed daub, stark as the Hermon snows at noon, turned back my gaze. Each dwelling stood a cube of clay, defined in knife-edge shadows by the sun's fierce glare. The rooftops and the courtyards showed no labour, whilst sightless windows told of dark interiors, all motionless and cool. Down in the dust a hen scratched viciously for fallen grain. Briefly, I viewed her struggle, then looked about me. I was a stranger; and yet the place somehow familiar. The moments passed. The silence and the stillness grew. 'Is this the house?' I wondered. The building had that vacant sense. It told me I had called in vain.

'If you're looking for old Amittai, then you'll find him up in the vineyards! "Truthful" that's what we call him here. It's the meaning of his name!' The woman's shout, in crudest Zebulun twang, went through me like a knife. Eyes had been watching after all, but neither face nor form appeared to claim the voice. Though glad to get the news, the chattering of the quiet siesta seemed almost sacrilege. Unobtrusively, I went, tip-toeing softly through the empty streets. I came to a fountain, refreshed myself with the sparkling water, then made my way to the hills where the vines stretched row on row to the cloudless sky. Amittai was fast asleep when I found him and I sat quietly, in the shade of a tree, till he awoke. He showed no visible surprise at my presence, almost as if I were part of his environment; as if there were something of myself in him; or something of himself in me.

'Wonderfully peaceful up here,' I ventured.

'Yes,' he said, 'but it wasn't always so, not even in my lifetime. You'd hardly believe it, but I've seen the day when you couldn't get to the fountain without getting an arrow in your back.' It seemed rather an abrupt beginning but I did not mind, so anxious was I to learn about the man I'd come to seek.

'You see,' he went on, 'the Syrians sent their bands all through these hills. Right down through Asher and Dan they came, and there was nothing we could do to stop them. Just helpless, that's what we were, like sparrows amongst the rocks, which the youngsters pick off with their stones. If it had gone on much longer, they'd have wiped us right out. I tell you there's many a woman still weeps for her man in the village. And some of the young fellows, "the cream of Israel", I called them, were speared to death in the scrub out there.' He paused awhile to make sure my eye found the spot, an arid region on the brow of the hill just above the vineyards. He sat very pensive and I rather doubted whether he would continue his story, then suddenly he spoke again.

'Do you know my boy?' he asked. 'Jonah's his name.'

'Well, I can't say I've met him,' I said, 'but I've heard plenty about him. His name's rather special isn't it?'

'Yes,' the old man replied, 'it means a dove . . . Aye,' he sighed, 'and it takes me back many a year. All's quiet in the valley now but in those days, life was chaos, there was no other word for it. When the Syrians came over the top, they were like demons let loose. All these vineyards have been planted since then, but when our boy was born, we hadn't a thing. Not a grape! And that's as sure as my name is Amittai!' And picking up a piece of rock, he threw it down the slope with a vehemence that startled me. 'So we called him Jonah. Perhaps you remember how Moses wrote in the Book of the Law about the world becoming empty and void, and how there was darkness on the face of the deep. I guess that's what we felt about Gath-Hepher in those terrible days. But Moses didn't stop there. He told also, how the Spirit of God brooded like a dove on the waters and how earth's light and life were born. It's a long while ago now to recapture one's emotions, but I think we

hoped our little "dove" would grow up to be a man of
God, filled with that same Spirit and that one day he might
show us a way out of the wreckage and darkness of our
village, into the sunshine again.'

'And he lived up to his name?' I asked hopefully.

'He did indeed,' replied Amittai staunchly. 'I hardly
like to say he took after his father, for his mother was a
good woman[2] but he grew up to be, not only a truthful boy,
but a boy who loved the Truth; and when I say that, I
mean he was taught of God, for he learned to speak of Him,
in a way I never did. But I must tell you what changed his
whole status here. At the time, the Syrian raids were especially bad, but on one particular day, during a lull in the
fighting, Jonah got the villagers together and spoke to us
all. Although I'm his father, I'd never heard him speak
like that. Why, the very authority of God was in his voice!
Don't ask me to repeat word for word what he said, but it
went something like this.'

The voice of the old man became reverent now, and his
words full of meaning. 'Thus saith the Lord,' he began,
'Jeroboam, the son of Joash, King of Israel, will restore all
Israel's frontiers, from the hill-pass of Hamath, right down
to the coast, for He has seen the affliction of Israel and He
knows the bitter times through which we pass. I will not
blot out Israel's name, saith the Lord, from under heaven..
I will save you by the hand of Jeroboam, the son of Joash.'[3]
He paused a moment, then continued in a more normal
tone, 'We all knew, of course, that Jeroboam was a godless
king and it baffled us how he could be God's instrument to
rout the Syrians but we certainly believed that God had
spoken, and that all He had said to us through Jonah would

[2] It has been suggested that Jonah's mother was the Shunammite and that
Jonah was her son, whom Elisha raised from the dead. Interesting though
this is in the light of Jonah's later experience and his significant foreshadow-
ing of the death and resurrection of Christ, this concept of his maternal
background cannot in actual fact, be substantiated from Scripture.

[3] See II Kings 14 v. 25–27.

B

be fulfilled. Then news of the prophecy came to the king
down south, at his palace in Samaria, and Jonah was sum-
moned to appear before him. After that, everyone in Israel
looked to Jeroboam for action. Stirred by the message and
urged on by the people, it wasn't long before his royal
battalions came marching through. Thrilling to see them,
it was, and to know the battle was not ours but God's. In
one way they seemed all too few, but God was with us and
we knew He would keep His word. What happened was
nothing short of a miracle. They drove the Syrian bandits
back through the defiles and hounded them from ridge
to ridge, until our men took the pass where all the land
fans out to Hamath. What's more, they've held it to this
day. We're clear now, right from the sea to Galilee. Just
mention Jonah down in the village. He's their hero; and
known too, all over Israel. I never thought a son of mine
would be a prophet; and it's not many prophets, you know,
who see their words fulfilled in their lifetime!' Then
his voice dropped as if he felt guilty of pride, and he
added reverently, 'But the kindness of the Lord is very
great.'

With this, Amittai rose to his feet and moved away to
attend to his vines. I followed him and as I did so, a vague
breeze went rustling through the leaves of the trees where
we had been sitting.

'Do you think I might see Jonah some day in Gath-
Hepher?' I enquired. A look of uneasiness crept over the
vinedresser's eyes, as if our conversation had been over-
heard, and neighbours had observed us. At first I could not
share his anxiety for I was filled with wonder, thinking how
the Creator of all things and the Inhabiter of Eternity, had
spoken His word through an inhabitant of this village. A
whole minute passed and I was conscious of a growing embarrassment. Amittai stood silent, not so much unwilling,
as unable to speak.

'Sorry,' I said, rather self-consciously, 'if it's not suitable, it doesn't matter.'

Sensing my disappointment, he said, 'No, it's not that, it's just that I don't know what to say.'

'About what?' I asked.

'About Jonah,' he blurted out and we stood silent again. 'You see, he's gone away.'

'But where?'

'I don't know,' he answered; 'not that that matters. After all, he's a grown man and a prophet, and I wouldn't expect him to tell me unless he felt he should, but it was the way he left. He was morose. Somehow, so changed. He's got money all right, all he'll need, I guess; but it was the look on his face . . . Almost as if he weren't a prophet any more.' For a moment or two he paused, then he said it again softly and with a sad far-away expression. 'That was it . . . almost as if he weren't a prophet any more.'

He had hardly finished speaking, when quite suddenly and without warning, the sun went in and we both looked up as one man. Thick clouds were gathering and gathering fast.

'Strange thing for this time of year,' I said, 'but it looks like a storm.'

'Aye,' he answered, 'it looks like a storm. And what do you make of that wind?' The fear in his voice struck at my heart. Hurriedly I started the descent, picking my way down through the stones of the watercourse, to the hamlet below. By the time I had reached Gath-Hepher, all was a raging fury of dust and sand . . .

Now it was time to turn the page once more, and as I did so, I was gripped by the words:

'Jonah rose up to flee unto Tarshish
from the Presence of the Lord . . .
But the Lord cast forth a great wind into the sea.'

CHAPTER 2

A POOL OF SLIME

Far to the east, where the life-line of the Tigris cuts a
swathe of green through the endless desert dunes, the eyes
of the Lord look down. The mystic Hiddekel, whose ancient
flow first took its rise in Eden, runs like a thread, on which
the beads of history tell their sordid tale . . . Resen, Dura,
Opis, Calneh, but still the mistress of them all is proud,
voluptuous Nineveh. Early in post-diluvian days, Asshur
laid its first foundations and through some fifteen hundred
years, it grew by toil and plunder, to an unthought fame;
a world metropolis, 'great before God', the fairest city built
on earth, since Cain first founded Enoch. Yet lower down
this same Hiddekel, stood Daniel in a later time, faced with
God's heavenly Man, His eyes aflame and girt with Uphaz-
gold. Such were those eyes that scanned the Tigris now,
searching its length and breadth, till fixed at last, upon
this centre of the pagan world.

Who had not heard of Nineveh, that dread epitome, yet
grand superlative of all mankind's achievements? Its name
and fear had reached to farthest frontiers; its power and
influence shadowed distant lands. For sixty miles the outer
ramparts stretched.[1] The inner walls rose heavenward, a

---

[1] Although the desolation of Nineveh was complete by Roman times,
Diorus Siculus of the first century BC, may well be citing an authentic tradi-
tion when he states that Nineveh formed a quadrangle, measuring a
hundred and fifty stadia by ninety; that is to say, it had a total perimeter of
four hundred and eighty stadia or about sixty miles. This agrees favour-
ably with the Biblical record, which describes Nineveh as 'a city of three
days' journey'; for if this refers to its circumference, it would mean that a
day's journey was about twenty miles, a normal reckoning in those days.
It has now been established that fortified habitation extended from Tarbisu,
a royal seat three miles north of Nineveh proper, southward along the River
Tigris to Biblical Calah, some twenty-one miles.

hundred feet;[2] and horse-drawn chariots, three abreast, could even ride its battlements. And higher still above this guardian-colossus, rose numerous towers, a hundred feet again. Within this vast perimeter, stretched endless palaces and grounds, parklands and pavements, homes and farms boasting a populace of half a million souls. The king's own residence,[3] emblem of tyranny and art, stood on a wide and elevated platform, viewing with arrogant disdain the humbler dwellings of the poor below. Its gardens, rooms and stately halls extended twenty-five full acres. Its base alone would take ten thousand slaves twelve years to build. And at its heart, the courtyard with its broad expanse, filled with a pageantry that spoke the glories of a world dominion. Huge pillars, each grotesquely carved with heads of men, winged bulls or lions, stood sentinel, as conquering generals and their wheeling troops streamed by in constant cavalcade before the emperor throne.

Yet like some sensuous harlot, decked with her finery and living in a luxury without peer, Nineveh, mistress of witchcrafts and seducer of mankind, sits on her perfumed bed. Into her lavish boudoir come, one upon another, the

[2] Archaeologists have managed to trace the main outline of the walls of the inner citadel of Nineveh. This part of the metropolis was approximately three miles long and slightly less than one and a half miles wide. The overall complex, however, included Calah some eighteen miles to the south, and the townships of Resen and Rehoboth-Ir. See Genesis 10 v. 11-12 for data on the origin of this ancient urban area.

[3] There are various palaces which have been excavated over the years in the general region of Nineveh. Two of the most famous mounds are known as Kuyunjik and Nabi Yunis on the River Tigris opposite Mosul, in present-day Iraq. The chief palace in existence when Jonah preached in Nineveh was probably that of Ashurnasirpal, 884-859 BC, a king whose name means, 'the god Asshur is guardian of the heir'. If this were so, Jonah would deliver his message some sixty to one hundred years after it was built. Its ruins are at Calah, the site of modern Nimrud, and indicate that its buildings alone occupied six acres. The renowned palaces of Sargon II, 721-705 BC, and Ashurbanipal, 668-631 BC, were, of course, erected at a later period. Whilst the description given in the text above is in certain respects typical of Assyrian palaces, the dimension and identity of the royal palace in Jonah's day remains a matter of conjecture.

merchant courtesans of her attendant nations. By whole-
sale 'whoredom', she has inveigled well-nigh every race into
her net. Her international commerce, holds in a vice-like
grip, the poor economies of her vassal states, till families,
nations, children, men, are sold at whim. Her sterile deities
spue forth their blasphemies from temple-courts that
counterfeit the Israel-sanctuary of God; and through the
then known world, the poison of her obscene culture
spreads. Lying and deceit her weapons; violence and
drunkenness her fruit; atrocity and outrage are her stock-
in-trade. She purrs in animal contentment, a lioness in her
lair, filled with her meat.

So to her voracious coffers, the wealth of countless
victims flows and loveless tribute from her subjects pours.
Booty of men and things, from cities sacked and blood-
stained battlefields, burgeon the fabled treasury, to glut
her vaults with gems and gold, till on the ruin of a myriad
souls, the opulence and unimagined splendour grows.
Thus, as to some strange pool of slime, whose depths are
sinister and unknown, the precious silt of rivers numberless, disgorge their wealth and filth to Nineveh. Foul then,
beyond degree, and rich beyond all computation, mighty,
magnificent, yet steeped in misery, her man-made majesty
rides on to judgement. The lavish courts, the royal prerogatives, the constant grandiose and bellicose display, the
rampant lust to conquer and to build, all floats upon the
stagnant ferment of a cesspool, devilishly vile.

This staggering stench of untold wickedness, reeks upward to the nostrils of the God in Heaven. His eyes look
down, those eyes that see the evil and the good; He, at the
apex of affairs, cognisant of a peasant's faith in old Gath-
Hepher, and knowing well the wilful evil of Assyria's
throne. These varied points form now, the operational
triangle of the God who reigns. His hand will reach from
heaven above to humblest Zebulun, and pit this tiny

countryman against the strongest potentate the world has known. The truth this boastful city needs is given to this village youth. The complex world of Nineveh, with all its ostentation, wealth and wisdom, must soon bow low before one simple sentence from the mouth of God. The shameless Gentiles with all their brash sophistication, must lick the dust, to own the word of one believing Israelite. This was the plan. Jehovah to Jonah; Jonah to Nineveh; then Nineveh to God. The act of grace would have no precedent. Now was the time, though no man knew it. The sin of Nineveh cried out for judgement. Her weeping sores, left unattended, would mar mankind beyond recall. Whilst evil mounts, the wisdom sown in Jonah's heart matures. Vessels of mercy and of wrath wait on the mingling of the Great Dispenser; the threads of judgement and of grace, the all-wise interweave of God. His is the apex-eye; the eye of Him who destines and divines, who sees and knows, yet stoops to save; who wielding things that are not, brings to nought the things that are.

And now the lightning missive strikes. God's fierce imperative goes forth to old Gath-Hepher. It is the hour. The Lord's decree, swift from His lips, speeds like an arrow to its mark. Jehovah-God commands Amittai's son. The rustic child to Nineveh must go, that sinful Ninevites won back to God, might in a later day rise up to judge those generations better blessed than they.

It is a total strategy that brings within its scope, the Jew, the Gentile and the Church of God; that sees its final fruit, when all mankind is bowed at last before God's Throne.

CHAPTER 3

THE JOPPA DILEMMA

Along the dusty southbound road, Jonah trudged slowly on, each step a confirmation of his will to leave. He talked to no-one; not even God. He felt too miserable for that. Why speak again, when all he had to say was spoken? The sun beat down upon him but he did not care. He was determined to go. He had made his decision and nothing would stop him. Once he had been well known. Now he would be unknown. But it was better that way. He would stand by his principles. The rough terrain dropped quickly to the coastal plain and the fresh sea-air relieved his burden. He would be in Joppa tomorrow, if all went well.

As soon as he arrived he went straight to the harbour. The bustling activity intrigued him after the sultry stillness of his village. How he marvelled at their energy and drive, as they shifted their wares, shouted their catch, mended their nets and loaded their ships. He felt tired, very tired, in fact well-nigh exhausted, but it was not the journey that wearied him and somehow he knew it. An early sailing might settle things. Perhaps he'd feel better when once he'd got going. He would start his enquiries.

This was the Japhia of Joshua's day, a landmark for the tribes, when dividing the land. It knew the business of the centuries. The ebb and flow of Gentile tides had weathered its stones, for Joppa was old already when Jonah walked its quays. Now in more recent times, this ancient port has come again to prominence. Its citrus fruits make Jaffa known in many a Gentile home, though few recall the things that happened there; things which have changed all history and effect us still.

And not for Jonah only did this seaport stand for crisis. Simon of Galilee, son of that later Jonah, saw conflict there. The burning issue proved identical. The same great question ravaged both their hearts. Paul sums it up for each of them. 'Is God the God of the Jews only, or God of the Gentiles also?'

Although for Paul, the Lord's commission embraced both Jew and Gentile, this was hardly the case with Jonah, or yet with Simon Peter. Only through crisis were they won to larger faith and bigger concepts of the God who loves the great Creator be, in fact, a tribal-god engaged in petty the prelude of His wider plan to save mankind. How could the great Creator be, in fact, a tribal-god engaged in petty feuding with the neighbouring clans?

Did He not say to Abraham, 'In thee shall *all the nations* of the earth be blessed'?

Had He not used the patriarch Joseph to feed *the world at large* with bread?

And though He set the nations' bounds with Israelitish destinies in view, it was *that men of every race* might seek Him too.

The temple at Jerusalem, whilst still Jehovah's dwelling place, inferred far more. It was a house of prayer for *all the nations.*

And as for Sheba's queen, she came from *Gentile Africa* to find God's blessing, in the words the son of David spoke.

Had Jonah never thought on this? And what of other prophets' ministry; the things *they* said and did?

Surely he knew that Israel's Lord once sent Elijah to Sarepta, that there a starving widow of Sidonia, might prove Jehovah's power and care?

Had he forgotten how the *Syrian,* Naaman, had found God's healing in obedience?

This love divine transcending Israel's frontiers was not unknown to his contemporaries.

Joel but recently had preached, 'Whoever calls on the Name of the Lord shall be saved.'

While Amos boldly spoke of heathen folk on whom God's Name was called.

And as for Hosea, the new emerging voice, he dared to claim that all those Gentiles, changed through grace, would be God's children.

Being the child of an insular society, Jonah lay captive behind the sullen walls of prejudice. He had succumbed to the malaise afflicting most of his compatriots. How swiftly spiritual distortion disqualifies God's chosen men! For some an empty ritualism stifles the upsurge of their joy. In others a pseudo-intellectualism poisons their earlier unfeigned trust in God. Exclusivism cruelly strangles living contacts and heedless liberalism, throws helpless sheep to ravening wolves. We flirt with fantasy. *We* are the 'heroes' and the 'martyrs' of our times, the 'sole' supporters of God's interest in our age. Critics are heretics. A blinding paranoia infects our witness, to show once more, that zeal bereft of knowledge, will crucify God's truth in any age. So do we choke those very channels through which God's love would flow.

This was the case with Jonah. The rime of national privilege grew thick within, till dangerously restrictive. God was so great and he so small. The pressure mounted but he would not yield. Though he himself was spiritually delinquent, he saw no problem. God's choice was Israel; He possessed her. God's hope was Israel; He would use her. God's reign on earth was vested in her. The nation's growth, prosperity and power were always therefore, His advantage!

But such slick reasoning had its flaws. All this was true if Israel worked in harmony with God. Then she would be His bridgehead in this rebel world, His chosen instrument to bless or judge the nations; yet as things stood, she flouted and despised the very One she claimed to serve. Jonah, rebellious and self-willed, was but a sample of his race. Prophet and nation were alike unsuited for their destined role.

When Jonah initially opposed the Nineveh commission, he spoke with deep emotion of 'my country'. He viewed his God as Israel's champion, who now was breaking faith with Israel's hopes. Jonah construes the covenant, then takes his God to task for not accepting his construction. Could anything be more obnoxious? Does God, who 'makes of man one blood', incite to racialism? True nationhood remains a gift from Him, an act of sovereign choice within His warp and woof of purpose. Each strand of race – white, black or coloured – must wait the final fabric, to perceive its relevance. Who are the empire builders? Gods or men? '*I* will make of thee,' God says to Abraham, 'a great nation.' So national greatness is not gained by crude assertion of our 'independence', nor yet through cries for self-determination. It lies in character; that moral stamp that marks the God-acknowledging, God-fearing and God-centred race. 'Righteousness,' the Bible says, 'is that which will exalt a nation,' not the massacre of the opposition or the genocide of racial minorities. Amalek aspired to nationhood apart from God, but note the verdict. 'Amalek was first of the nations;[1] but his latter end shall be that he perish for ever.' If Israel, appointing her own king, exerting her own strength and fighting her own battles, does so for her own ends, and to uphold her own supremacy, then God's Name, idly bandied on her lips, will not save her from destruction. Men and nations are divine means, not human ends; vehicles only, not objectives.

If the thing formed exerts a claim, it falls apart. Only as

[1] Some consider that Numbers 24 v. 20 refers to Amalek being the first to oppose Israel after the exodus, rather than elucidating the chronology of her ethnic origin.

malleable can mankind be serviceable. In our availability to God is found our credibility of being. Only by dint of function do we foil futility and act responsibly. How good to know that God is patient and exceeds our understanding. 'He shall not fail or be discouraged.' Time and Eternity are on His side and they are inexorable. Though Jonah flees in protest, God is frighteningly inclusive. 'The publicans and the harlots,' said Jesus, 'go into the kingdom of God before you.' And how the Pharisees rejected that, the Cross bears witness!

Our Lord was always a Samaritan to orthodoxy, for he cared more for individual people than their empty institutions. Each man who works with Him will know His Joppa. Enlargement or redundancy remain the stark alternatives. Is it not challenging to find, that both Jonah and Bar-Jonah, were, in this self-same port, confounded by The Greater Love?

How wide the mercies of the God of Israel! How small our faith who set His measure in mere catalogues and creeds!

CHAPTER 4

THE CHOSEN VESSEL

As Jonah wandered through the piles of tackle, the heaps
of produce and the numerous shacks that littered the jetties
of Joppa, his mind seemed equally cluttered. Not that he
had any desire to set things in order but rather to clear his
decks, and hoist his mainsail while the winds of passion
still were blowing. There were all kinds of boats moored
in the harbour but most were scheduled for coastal runs,
either southward to Philistia or northwards to Phoenician
Tyre. Some perhaps were bound for Cyprus but even that
was rather close for what he had in view. He had come to
Joppa *incognito*. Discovery would spoil his plans. They
would want him to say something and his very silence
would arouse suspicion. If only he could find a berth on an
ocean-going vessel. His eyes looked out beyond the maze
of masts and rigging, to the far horizon. Strange how his
love for Israel should somehow drive him from it. That
was the irony. The hurt went deeper every hour.

At last he found the looked-for craft. There it lay,
heaving on the tide, low in the water, and soon to sail. He
hastily pursued his purpose and found, to his satisfaction,
it was bound for Tarshish. The place was a synonym in
the Hebrew mind for distance, the final outpost of
Phoenician trade, far to the west where the sun went down.
This was the voyage 'schoolboys' dreamed of, as drowsily
they conned their scrolls and intoned the Law. It spoke of
the ends of the earth and for this very reason would serve
him well. Now was the moment of decision. What should
he do? Fortified by proud resentment, he stepped on
board.

And where after all might Tarshish be? Was it Tartessus of the coasts of Spain, known for its iron and tin, its lead and silver plate? Or was it found in Honadu,[1] that continent beyond the sun-drenched capes of Africa? It did not matter. No sense of thrill stirred in his breast. Impassively he watched the silver pieces weighed. The distance, not the destination, was his real concern. Before him lay the longest journey man could make. It is so still, for any who would flee from God!

Slowly the balance lifted. Yes, it was costly, perhaps more costly than he knew. Why is it, if we cannot serve *our* way, we will not serve at all? We talk of conscience and conviction, but often are the victims of conceit. What of his baggage? It seemed so little – though it weighed so much. He had one piece, his case for leaving. It was enough, since all he had was packed within it.

The road that led to Joppa's quay was, like the Tigris, a twisted strand of history. To trace it back will tell us much of Jonah's problem. Amittai's boy was born, as far as 'The Books of the Kings' reveal,[2] in the reign of Jehoahaz, son of choleric Jehu, the one-time despot of the break-away tribes. The reign of Jehoahaz, which lasted seventeen years, was notorious for the Syrian incursion.[3] Led by their chieftain, Hazael, they plundered and pillaged Israel's northern frontiers, a scourge, no doubt, from Jehovah on the corrupt administration, though it was tempered with mercy. After his death, his son Jehoash[4] succeeded him, but he was a ne'er-do-well and only endorsed his father's abuses. Nevertheless, when Elisha lay critically ill, he paid him a visit, whether by reason of superstition or on account of divine constraint, who can tell, but the outcome was significant,

[1] An ancient name for India, though it is doubtful whether the Cape route was known to the Phoenicians.

[2] See the historical sequence of II Kings 13 v. 14 to 14 v. 29.

[3] See II Kings 13 v. 4.

[4] Also spelt Joash.

for the last word of the prophet disclosed the future of the war with Syria. The story itself is particularly poignant.

The king is sitting at the bedside, when Elisha calls for a bow and insists that an arrow be strung. The window is opened and the prophet's hands, made strong with the arms of God, take hold on the hands of his sovereign. 'Shoot!' he commands, and they watch the arrow take its flight, till it falls at last, in the dry brown grasses. 'The arrow of the Lord's deliverance!' cries Elisha, 'and the arrow of deliverance from Syria, for thou shalt smite the Syrians in Aphek, till thou hast consumed them! Now take the arrows,' he adds, 'and strike the ground.' At this the king is mystified, but lifts the quiver, and taps the floor halfheartedly three times. Suddenly a look of anger flushes the ailing prophet's face, 'You should have done that five or six times,' he says. 'Then you would have done the same to Syria and utterly defeated them; but now, three raids will mark the limit of your victory.' The king sits silent and displeased. Lethargic and licentious, he loathed enthusiasm. The dying prophet had discerned his man.[5]

As Jonah grew to manhood, through all those trying years, no doubt this death-bed scene became a byword with his people. Three times Jehoash forced the Syrians back, but as foretold, this was the end of his defensive forays. With vehement faith, he might have launched a full-scale onslaught, and by it freed his race from fear, but as it was, he died, and still the fifth and sixth attacks were wanting. It was evident the king had failed but did not God still mean to triumph? The 'arrow of the Lord's deliverance' had sped. Should it not find its mark in Syria? The fifth and sixth encounters must be made and Jonah knew it. The light of God lit up the crisis. They must fight on and certain victory would follow. With confidence he speaks his celebrated prophecy. King Jeroboam,[6] the heir of Jehoash,

[5] See II Kings 13 v. 14–20.   [6] i.e. King Jeroboam II.

surprisingly responds. The people rise and before the arrow of Jehovah, the Syrians fall, a vanquished foe.

Hence Jonah's notoriety quite early in his ministry. But though so quickly come to status, his inner stature could not match it. He was so young; the time too soon. Great in the eyes of men, he must grow greater in the eyes of God. The One who was greater than Jonah had chosen to en-large him; and like many another, it left him greatly dis-concerted. The call to Nineveh, though couched in terms of judgement, implied the hope of causeless grace. It took him out beyond his frontiers, in ways he did not care to think. Noah's world was judged by water, when they spurned his warning; and Sodomites by fire, when heedless of the character of Lot. If Nineveh refused the God-given word, no doubt His overthrow would purge them, and who would care? But Jonah sensed the unpredictable. God's love was so 'irrational'. It worked both ways. For not by merit had the Israelites possessed the Land, nor for their national righteousness, had Syria so lately been subdued. With moral failure prevalent, it was extraordinary that God should grant a victory. The prophet's strange mis-givings had foundation.

Some few months later, when Nineveh lay basking in God's sunshine, Jonah renewed his earlier complaint. 'O Lord,' he says, 'was not this my saying in my country? Therefore I fled before unto Tarshish, for I knew that Thou art a gracious God, and merciful, slow to anger and of great kindness and repentest Thee of the evil.' With such foreboding had he viewed the great commission. What would it mean? A prophecy of judgement unfulfilled? This chagrin, he might possibly endure. But what would happen to the nation? No doubt it was the sad beginning of the end. If Syria's commandoes left their bitter scars, a Nineveh preserved, would one day fiendishly destroy. And should he favour nations, which God might later use to flay his own? The maddening contradictions mounted in his heart; then one by one he firmly fixed them on his Lord. Jonah's concern was not with the lost or how to save them, but with a senseless urge to make his God concede his prejudice. The inconsistencies he raised, he would not reckon as his own. Let God Himself resolve the paradox, then he would serve. This was 'the graven image' he had fashioned. He trod the road that leaders tread to blasphemy. Once 'God' is moulded to our likeness, He stands no bigger than ourselves. Then, though we still may call him God, we act as lord.

Had Jonah lived to hear Isaiah preach, how shattered would his arguments have been. 'God of the whole earth, shall He be called,' such is Isaiah's claim. He dares to cry on His behalf, 'Look unto me and be ye saved all the ends of the earth.'

God after all, is infinite, not only in the extent of His being but in the qualities of His character. Like Jonah we may accept this as a theological abstraction, but shun its real and practical implications. God's purposes of love, like deep resistless rivers, run out from Israel to an ocean past all comprehension. The course of history reveals how quickly local politics can blur our eyes. As formerly explained, in showing first His grace to Israel, God planned to use this chosen nation to bring His blessing to mankind. Man's narrow thinking could not stop Him, nor could His great intention fail, when Israel turned apostate. The centuries show that even in their murder of Messiah, the wider purposes of love broke through to bring salvation to the world. Nor are His ancient people cast forever from His sight. By saving men from every race through Jesus, whom they crucified, corrupted Jewry sees today, a varied people, one in Christ. What Israel lost through unbelief, converted pagans of the Gentiles gained. The blessings of the eternal covenant flow on, whilst Israel stands bewildered and out-

c

raged. Yet this is also God's compassion. By such events He means to stir them from their torpor. In love, He longs to save them still. Had He not told them so? 'I will provoke you to jealousy by them that are no people and by a foolish nation will I anger you.'[7]

But even yet, we do not glimpse the ultimate of grace? If Israel's fall be proved a blessing to a myriad souls, what will accrue when wayward Israel turns to God and owns the Crucified as King? Surely the bringing to millennial peace, of men and nations numberless. For if their casting off was reconciliation for the world, what shall their last reception be, but life triumphant from the dead!

God meant the prophet and his nation to be as fresh as Galilee, that lake, whence living waters flowed; but now they were a Dead Sea, a religious cul-de-sac, a brackish tarn in which a bitter faith forbade God's living things to grow. The oracles, the covenants, the Christ Himself, were only Israel's glory as they brought the Gentiles light. But now she coveted a glory all her own. Her self-advancement was the *raison d'être* for her religion; and truth, the fettered servant of the ends of state. Her ultimate morality was measured by those acts which fostered national power. Such is the great delusion. Beneath these concepts Ninevites must die to make the Israelites secure. The innocent must perish with the guilty and keep the privileged enthroned. And so at last the wily Caiaphas maintained, it was expedient one man should die, else place and nation would be forfeit. The greatest evils clamour always for the 'highest good'. Men kill with ease once they can kill for 'God' and do 'Him' service! So precious things are counted vile in church and party and saints are branded heretics and rogues. The 'holiest' and hardest men, too often, are identical. Once dedication is perverted, it proves the biggest killer of them all. The zeal that makes men popes

[7] Romans 10 v. 19; 11 v. 11 and 14.

and potentates is that which ultimately destroys. Both Saul and Stalin murdered for 'the common good'. The Pharisee, the communist, theist and atheist, all serve the devil well. It must be so, once we believe ourselves and worship gods our little minds have made.

In countless things we still act Jonah-like today. Our church ideals play counterpart to Israel in the mind, and many other loyalties too. These entities for us are Christianity, the symbols of achievement in the realm of 'truth'; and be their circles wide or small, they are our progeny. Flesh of our flesh, their fortunes move us. To uphold and maintain them, extend and proclaim them, becomes our passion and our one crusade. Then suddenly, like Jonah we are caught off-guard. God gives us something else to do, but His commission breaks our own poor concept of His Person. Our work was 'His', yet now His work extends beyond us. Our understanding of the Truth we somehow viewed as Truth itself. Our little 'piece' of God was God 'entire'. Fresh vistas then, are suspect and unworthy of the 'piece' we know. Our 'hallowed' name and group security resist intrusion. The frontier posts 'our faith' defends, must be inviolate. We fret and fume if once the Living Lord confronts us. So Jonah packs his bag and goes. The case is closed. Like us, he knows the god he wishes to believe.

See how he mounts the gang-plank and that fare is paid. The price will follow. No other passenger appears. He goes alone. The captain has no qualms. The anchor weighs.

Who could have known the man from Zebulun would sink her? That all were doomed . . .

But for God's grace.

II

JONAH AND THE GREAT WIND

THE BOOK OF JONAH

Chapter 1 v. 4–11

But the LORD sent out a great wind into the sea, and there was a mighty tempest in the sea, so that the ship was like to be broken.

Then the mariners were afraid, and cried every man unto his god, and cast forth the wares that were in the ship into the sea, to lighten it of them. But Jonah was gone down into the sides of the ship; and he lay, and was fast asleep.

So the shipmaster came to him, and said unto him, What meanest thou, O sleeper? Arise, call upon thy God, if so be that God will think upon us, that we perish not.

And they said every one to his fellow, Come, and let us cast lots, that we may know for whose cause this evil is upon us. So they cast lots, and the lot fell upon Jonah.

Then said they unto him, Tell us, we pray thee, for whose cause this evil is upon us; What is thine occupation? And whence comest thou? What is thy country? And of what people art thou?

And he said unto them, I am an Hebrew; and I fear the LORD, the God in heaven, which hath made the sea and the dry land.

Then were the men exceedingly afraid, and said unto him, Why hast thou done this? For the men knew that he fled from the presence of the LORD, because he had told them.

Then said they unto him, What shall we do unto thee, that the sea may be calm unto us? For the sea wrought, and was tempestuous.

CHAPTER 5

OUTWARD BOUND

The minutes pass and the lumbering vessel noses its way forward to the widening sea. The sun drops slowly beyond the purple bands of night and as the stars peep out, the wash and wake glow phosphorescent in the gloaming. He is going forth to the darkness, whose word should have shown men the light.

But what said Moses when he blessed the tribes? 'Rejoice, O Zebulun, in thy going out!' Yet now the low-set, flat-roofed dwellings slip from his view, and with the twilight, a mist of gloom envelops Jonah's soul. Not only Gath-Hepher but the hamlet of Nazareth, lay hidden amongst the Zebulun hills. How different was the way of Messiah! 'His goings forth were from everlasting.' His one delight was His Father's will. With what joy He declared Him. He was the Bridegroom gone forth from His chamber. The Strong Man rejoicing to run in the race. Jonah went forth overshadowed by anger. The blessing was lost and the promise abandoned. His footsteps had faltered in the ebb of the tide.

Centuries later on the sunlit rooftops, Simon Peter (as we have seen), son of a later Jonah, fought out the same fierce issues. Joppa changed but little through the years. 'What God hath cleansed, call not thou common!' God's voice had spoken once; and now He spoke the second time. 'Arise . . . and go . . . and nothing doubting!' Peter obeys. The spell is broken. The Gospel of the Blessed God begins to set the Gentiles free. But Jonah broods. For him the second word has not been given. It is not time. God's work within him must be done, before God's work, by means of him, proceeds. The sign and preaching must be one. No way of ease can bring him now to harmony with God. Short cuts to destiny, unfailingly short-circuit power. Divine dimensions do not shrink through our imaginings. He is 'The Same'. If once we cast Him in a lesser mould, or 'dwarf' His deity, 'tis we, ourselves, who look ridiculous. We men of Jonah's ilk must change, not God, who calls us to His service. His character endures. Ours is the crisis. We may be casual, but He, in seriousness, will search us. His set appointments hold no options. God's gifts and callings stand for ever. When He, the Greater speaks, then we the lesser must obey. Our God persists. His will prevails. He knows no final dereliction of His plans.

This witness to God's sovereignty is plain. It is the Truth that dominates the book. Initiative belongs to God. So do prerogatives. As our Creator, He ever stands, our Antecedent. His will must always ante-date our own. By His decree our own responsibility is measured. Although prescribed, He makes it real, nor will He let it be negated. Jonah stands chosen in God's purposes but carnal concepts warp his choice. God's weight of mercy fills his cup. His vessel cracks. He pouts and panics, rants and runs. The interim is choked with reasoning, but final words belong to God. He fled the One who held the answer; and must return to find his peace.

Relentlessly his Lord pursues. Love never fails. The Word *of* God is ever with him, the Law and somewhat of The Writings too. Objectively, it forced no crisis. It was the word *from* God that shattered him; the Word *without* become God's word within. As living seed, it broke the ground it grasped. Detached, the prophet was unmoved, but once involved, the storm began. The gale that blew in old Gath-Hepher, attained its climax out at sea. It was the Lord who mounted such disturbance; His word and wind, that challenged conscience and conceptions. The Lord it is, who rules the pagans' lot; the Lord, who brings His monster from the deep to swallow, keep and finally disgorge His wilful child. Each element divinely ordered and employed, serves in its time and place, the destined end. The preparations of the Lord grant no escaping.

And even when the work of Jonah seems complete, God's work on Jonah still goes on. It is the Lord's east wind that wilts him; the Lord's fresh gourd that gives relief; and lastly, God's appointed worm that brings him to despair. Such are His ways to make men trust Him only. So do the 'all things' of the natural sphere serve God's good goal to bring men to His likeness. This is the alchemy divine, that makes of clay a thing of gold. Once called according to the purpose of our God, then all in heaven and earth is for us, grist for His mills, which, though they grind exceeding small, make us the finer for the Master's use. The wind and sun, the wave and flow; fish, flowers and men, are all His servants to the sovereign end. Such is His way through all the years. Such is His kindness in the seas. He is much nearer than we think although His footsteps are not known.

And so His voice sighs sadly through the rigging. There is His mourning in the chill night breeze. Beyond the flap, flap, flap of canvas, the Lord of earth and sea is speaking.

> 'O whither will you go . . .
> And whither will you flee . . . ?'

But Jonah stands in silence on the deck. His lips are closed, yet soon must answer. So shall the ancient words be spoken,

> 'If I ascend up into heaven
> Thou are there.
> If I make my bed in hell
> Thou are there.
> If I take the wings of the morning

And dwell in the uttermost parts of the sea,
Even there
Shall Thy hand lead me,
And Thy right hand shall hold me.
Yes, even there . . .
                    even there . . .
                              even there.'[1]

CHAPTER 6

THE DOVE ON THE DEEP

The land lies barely discernible, a dark thin line on the eastern horizon. A few brief moments and the deepening night must claim it for ever. The last reminder of the glorious past will then have yielded to the sordid 'now'. His was a one-way ticket without plans for return, yet high above, in quiet formation, the birds are homing on the wing. They know their time and place of rest. Did Jonah see them ere he went below?

Through all the barren highlands west of Jordan, the little rock-dove was endemic. How often as a boy, he must have found their eggs along the cliffs and gullies of Gath-Hepher. Yet here was a 'dove' upon the deep, a tattered, soiled and 'silly dove', to use Hosea's words for Ephraim, fleeing from Jehovah's Presence.[1] What purpose now, that special name he bore? Had it no meaning? The Spirit of God and the spirit of man are both portrayed by the dove in Scripture. Which content for his name would Jonah choose? Would he, like Noah's dove, returning to the ark, proclaim the assuaging of God's wrath? It seemed most doubtful and yet what hopes God placed in Jonah, this bearer of His dove-like name. He yearned, through Jonah, to brood upon those deeps of Nineveh and bring His peace where all was ruin and decay . . .

But God's ambassador had turned escapist. He makes the psalmist's sigh his own.

> 'O for the wings of a dove,' he cries,
> 'That I might fly away and be at rest.'

[1] Hosea 7 v. 11–13.

That was his sentiment. The chosen carrier had absconded. God's bird had flown.

In this decision the prophet's choice was out of character. 'Harmless as doves' the servants of the Lord should be, but Jonah's absence from his post was perilous, both for the men on board, and those in Nineveh awaiting doom. A disobedient man soon proves disastrous, for no-one lives to self alone. Rebellion tends to hurt the innocent, and one man's sin still fills the world with heart-break. A dove is gentle, we are told, because it has no gall; a symbol of contention from the earliest times. Mingled with vinegar, men proffered gall to Jesus, and not a few still do the same. It is a bitter thing, the spirit of self-will, bereft of any gentleness from heaven. Thus unamenable to God, the prophet grows unsociable with men. Addiction to a loveless faith will always isolate, then finally destroy. Tarshish means 'hard', and not without significance. Its trade was in hard metals and its life hard-bargaining, and Jonah, had he reached there, might well have been as hard as they. His current temper made him more an ostrich than a dove, for 'she leaves her eggs in the sand,' says the Scripture, 'and is hardened against her young.' Such was 'the way out' for Jonah and as always, it proved 'the way down'. It was so with Cain. 'My sin is too great to be forgiven!' he cries, and out he goes from the Presence of the Lord. It was so with Gehazi, who covetous and leprous, recoiled from the presence of his master. It was so with Judas who went out to the night. Of each of these it is written, 'he went out'; nor did a single one return. It is the way of the murderer, the liar and the traitor. It is the company we keep as soon as we go forth from God. It brings us to the dread descent where Satan's depths await us. 'Cast Thyself *down*!' says Satan to Jesus in the wilderness. 'Fall *down* and worship me!' he dares to ask, 'All shall be Thine!' Then on the Hill he strikes again. 'Come *down*,' he cries, 'Come *down* from

the cross!' It is the hallmark of our foe. Satan went forth
from God and down he fell from his primordial estate.
Now he would lead all God-forsakers, outwards and downwards to those fires prepared. It makes us tremble as we
think on Jonah's course. 'He went down to Joppa,' runs
the story, 'and found a ship.' 'He went *down* into it,' the
word continues; and finally we learn, 'he went *down*, even
to the sides of the ship.' Soon he would go down to 'the
bottom of the mountains', till out of the depths he cried
again to his Lord.

But this is not all. Let it be noticed, that in going *out*
from God's Presence and in going *down* to Joppa, he chose
to go '*with them*' to Tarshish. These too, are frightening
words, although today, to be 'with them' or even 'it' is
counted wise. It was when Judas 'stood with them', he
kissed and sold his Master; when Peter 'stood with them',
that he failed Him at the fire.[2] Our journeys and the
world's soon run together, if once our fellowship with God
is broken. Religious life divorced from God so quickly
makes the secular its mate. Did not the priests court Roman
power to send their critics to the tree? The social set-up
of our times suits well the purpose of declining saints. The
devil's boats still run for those who flee from God, especially
when we pay in silver. So out he goes; and down; and
under, who went 'with them'.

And so at last to sleep, the long deep sleep of one who
has finished talking; who weakened by the battle and the
ultimate defiance, sinks to oblivion, amidst the aftermath
of crisis. The privacy is sweet. He is his own, but God
looks on. 'A silly dove and without heart.' This is His
verdict. Love will not spare. 'For when you go, I'll spread
my net for you ... Woe unto you ... I will chastise you ...
You who have fled from me.'[3] A rude awakening lies in
store and God's own 'monster' in the deep.

[2] John 18 v. 5 and 18.　　　　[3] Hosea 7 v. 11–13.

Whatever be our thoughts of Jonah we should not make him too naïve. His own confession tacitly admits, he feared the Lord, the Maker of the sea and land. Not for one moment did he think the omnipresence of his God had lapsed, or that His known omnipotence had ceased. Ironically, God's omnipresence rarely scares us. Such grand diffusion, puts us rather at our ease. Or so we think! In this we all are animists at heart. The great Creator is benevolent! His love is everywhere! He'll do no harm! It is the demons that are dangerous; so with a fetish, bribe or favour we constantly appease the adverse spirit, man or thing. But when the God of *everywhere* becomes particular, and He who made us, finds us *somewhere*, terror fills us. We fear for everything but Him, until He meets us face to face. Though immanence has wonder, it is Immanuel who makes Him real. The God of glory always lights those men He uses. He blinds them ere He makes them see. By personal confrontation, the patriarchs and prophets found their faith, and such as Saul were changed to Paul. The universal Power, men universally admit; but in His *personal* Presence, do they live or wither, bow or flee.

For Jonah, in his desperate disagreement, Joppa was the Great Divide. Eastward there lay the Land, the Israelite's inheritance; westward, the seething ocean of the Gentile world. Long years before, both Hiram and King Solomon had viewed it so. 'We will bring the wood in floats by sea to Joppa,' suggested the King of Tyre, 'and thou, O Solomon shall carry it to Jerusalem.' As far as Jonah's nation was concerned, east of Joppa, God was present; westward, 'merely' omnipresent. The Land to the Jew was, in a special sense, where God was found. In Moses' words, it was a land for which the Lord God cared. 'His eyes are upon it,' he said, 'from the beginning of the year, even unto the end of the year', those eyes that see the evil and the good. Through all the passing seasons, therefore, the Israelites were made to feel that close behind the visible authorities, there reigned the Great Ordainer of them all, with whom they really had to do. The constant sight of priests and Levites, the varied festivals from month to month, the reading of the Law in home and concourse; the ministry of prophet, seer and sage, all these together with the sanctuary in Zion, made being in the Land a real experience of God. This was the sphere in which Jehovah made Himself particularly answerable to Israel; the sphere in which they also, were particularly answerable to Him.

Nor were these concepts fond subjective notions arising from their supernatural past. Joshua's description still informed them. 'This,' he declared, 'is the land of the possession of the Lord, wherein the Lord's tabernacle dwelleth.' The Land and the Presence were therefore co-extensive in the minds of the people. Such concepts were current in the days of Jehoahaz, when, in all probability, Jonah was born. The inspired commentary on the period reads like this 'The Lord was gracious unto them . . . and would not destroy them, neither cast them *from His Presence*.'[4] But later, when Judah grew spiritually bankrupt and their removal from the Land was imminent, God says of King Zedekiah, 'he did that which was evil in the sight of the Lord . . . for through the anger of the Lord, it came to pass in Jerusalem and Judah, until He had cast them *out of His Presence*.'[5] This mode of expression is confirmed also by Jeremiah. God says in his prophecy, 'Behold I, even I, will utterly forget you and I will forsake you and the city that I gave you and your fathers, and cast you *out of My Presence*.'[6, 7]

All down history this is something Israel's enemies have

[4] II Kings 13 v. 22–23.   [5] II Kings 24 v. 20.   [6] Jeremiah 52 v. 3.
[7] H. Martin in his *The Prophet Jonah* especially deals with this.

refused to acknowledge. They have been saying for centuries and still say today, 'Come and let us cut them off from being a nation; that the name of Israel may be no more in remembrance.'[8] Ezekiel takes the measure of this attitude when he writes, 'Thou hast said, these two nations (i.e. Judah and Israel) and these two countries shall be mine and we will possess it; whereas the Lord was there.'[9] Whatever the councils of men may decree about Palestine, Jehovah remains its custodian. He is to be reckoned with, there on that patch of hills and valleys, lakes and plains.

This was precisely the position with Jonah. He knew full well that whilst God was everywhere, the experience of 'Jehovah Shammah'[10] was inescapable in the Land. 'The Lord was there.' It was this continual sense of personal confrontation, that was so unbearable to him in his defiant state of mind. He had refused his Master's orders, and now he would go where he need not face Him in every stick and stone. The Land as far as Jonah was concerned was his sphere of employment. He, himself, stood stubbornly opposed to transfer, and yet his master would not take his resignation. It was an *impasse*. If service in the Land were unacceptable, then he was through; let God pursue him as He would. So he had quit and now the Presence faded from him as the shore-line passed from view . . .

And if today, at distance from the work of God, we lie inactive and asleep, the prophet's case will find us out. A church where Christians gather in Christ's Name is like the Land. There, in Himself, the riches of the saints' inheritance are found. Where two or three are gathered thus, the promise tells them that 'the Lord is there'. His Presence is particularly real. They sense Him in His

---

[8] Psalm 83 v. 4.   [9] Ezekiel 35 v. 10.
[10] It means, 'The Lord is there'. Ezekiel 48 v. 35.

people, ordinances and Word and know His nearness in the praise and prayer. It is within the Christian company that Christ so readily confronts us, and the Spirit's voice is heard. But if we will not listen or obey; if we forsake the true assembling of the saints and thus 'get out', the walk-out with superior air, too often means we flee the Lord. And though we raise a thousand reasons, it is His gaze we cannot meet. His Presence rankles. His handling of the issues is at 'fault'. That is 'the cause', and so we go.

But should not Joppa and its crisis check us ere we put to sea? It is a lovely place. Why make it memorable with tragedy and grief? Its meaning speaks of 'height' and 'beauty'. Why leave the highest and loveliest to flounder in the deep. 'Honour and majesty are before Him: strength and beauty are in His sanctuary.' In one sense, all the land was that, to pious Jews. As found in Dan, port Joppa raises, too, the question of contrasting destinies. 'Dan shall judge his people,' said Jacob, 'as one of the tribes of Israel.' 'Dan is a lion's whelp,' added Moses, 'he shall leap from Bashan.' Right decisions at Joppa can lastingly affect our work and witness. But Jacob shows Dan's other nature. 'He shall be as a serpent by the way,' he prophesies, 'an adder in the path, that biteth the horse's heels, so that his rider shall fall backward.' With Jonah, the serpent of Dan, and not the lion, had triumphed at Joppa. His ministry could have been so regal, authoritative, supple and far-reaching, but now he acts as a 'narrow snake', to use the marginal rendering, and a creeping thing. He is a danger to all, lurking like a reptile in the bowels of the ship. Such is the challenge of Jonah's crisis. Although he believed, he still chose the low dark way from Joppa's heights.

There in his bunk he lay, so quiet and still; yet on the sea outside, the rising wind drove ugly furrows through

D

the water's face. When brooding as the dove of peace, what heavenly calm the Spirit brings, but as the hurricane of God, the cedars splinter and the ocean heaves, so now the wind that stirred in Jonah's birth place, sweeps seaward to the man himself. It is Jehovah's wind, even that east wind of destruction 'that breaketh the ships of Tarshish'. All that God touches as the narrative proceeds, bears out His greatness. This is a 'great wind' and arouses a 'great tempest'. Jonah is swallowed by a 'great fish'. He speaks to a 'great city', and witnesses at last the 'great kindness' of Him who is so infinitely greater than Jonah. 'God is great,' says Elihu, 'but He maketh small . . .' This action Jonah soon must prove and prove it to the full. Yes, he had been somebody and soon he would be nobody, but as a result, become a blessing to everybody. He had deceived himself, but when God's work in Jonah had been done, he would be a sign from the deep to save men from the ultimate deep. Saved from a physical death in the seas of time he would save men from a spiritual death in the Lake of Fire. God's sovereignty will never wantonly destroy us. It shows us only, the Almightiness of Him who holds our hand.

Ninevite folk-lore already spoke of a god-like emissary, who would come from the sea. It linked with Dagon, the half-fish, semi-human idol of Assyria the Philistines once worshipped. Would now another come to teach them from the deep? This time a figure, not of myth and legend, but the messenger of God?

CHAPTER 7

STORM AND SLUMBER

The captain stands alone, his hands upon the helm. He is feeling his way through the growing storm. He is distinctly uneasy, for used though he is to the sea and the sky, this gale has struck without warning. The rollers already are lifting high and the primitive craft wallows clumsily in the menacing swell. The sky is black. The wind hums wildly through the ropework and the biting spray whips in his face like a lash in the galleys. He can delay no longer. Crisply, he barks his orders. 'Shorten sail,' he shrieks, with hands cupped tensely round his lips. The crew go scurrying to their stations, and still his eyes fix on the swirling current and the curling breakers. Things could hardly be worse. The prow dips downwards, lost in a yawning trough of eddying water, then up it shoots on the bosom of the deep, to meet the white-foamed anger. The rise and fall increase in violence. The decks below the fo'c'sle are awash. The danger mounts. On every side dark pyramids of heaving ocean wait to engulf them. They plunge again. He feels the vessel shudder beneath the weight of water, then cleave the surface like a monster mad for air. Time and again the seething seas relent, to fall cascading from her bows. How long the ship can stand such pounding, he dare not think. Meanwhile the sodden timbers creak and groan as if the death throes of the vessel have begun.

The darkening sky seems darker still. The night has come, maybe for ever. One thing is certain. The work to lighten her must start or not a man will see the dawn. The task is nothing but a death-dance. Drenched by the endless ebb and flow, the aching hands ease heavy bales up from below, then slowly to the parapets, where toppled by their weight, they plummet stone-like to the depths below.

Distraught, the captain struggles with the tiller. He knows full well the odds his men are facing. Conditions worsen. It is a hurricane they ride. His hopes recede. When would the vessel yield? Was all the cargo lost in vain? And still he waits. At times, an agonising cry leaps through the howling tempest to his ears. He understands and feels it too. There is a Presence in the storm, an unknown element behind the fury of the night. Baalim! Astarte! Asherah! O that the gods might rise and save them! Or were they so outraged, their malevolence sought now to drown them. Another desperate hour goes by. The gale still rages, but then, for once, the boat is handling. This is the looked-for moment. He leaves the mate to man the helm and slips below. No thought of rest comes to his mind. He has his theory. Be what it may; god, man or demon, find it he must. His urge is frantic, for should he fail, he feels the fate of all is sealed.

Exhausted from his long exertion, he staggers downwards to the hold, fastening the hatches as he goes. He lifts the lantern from its hook and starts his search. The ship reels drunkenly from port to starboard. Although so many years at sea, he finds it hard to keep erect. Precariously, he lurches through the cargo space, and out along the shadowy catwalks. The bilge slops ankle-deep around him. The rats are restless. He even feels them brush his legs, whilst scampering to and fro. He comes now to the framework of the ship. Between the inner boarding and the hull are numerous berths, much like those found in smaller fishing-smacks today. He scans the crew's effects but finds no answer. He passes on to where the occasional passenger might rest. The noise is deafening. The flickering lamp casts eerie fingers back and forth. They stab the gloom with sickly light. The captain stiffens. In one brief flash, he sees a hunched-up form, a sleeping shape within the shadow of a bunk-hole. He is astounded. Indeed it angers him, that anyone could dream his way through such a crisis. 'Wake up!' he roars. 'The boat's away, and *you* asleep! What do you mean! Listen!' he shouts, then pauses. The crunch of wood on wood comes snarling through the storm. It sounds as if her back is breaking and with fresh urgency he shouts again. 'Wake up! Wake up! Call on your God, maybe He'll save us yet.' The captain turns. The darkness swallows him; then strange forebodings grip the prophet. It is the Lord who roars without. The fury that devours has found him now.

In one of those rare lulls that mark the very wildest weather, the crew assemble for a meal. Some feel too ill to eat and most can only snatch a bite, then hurry back to man their posts. Tersely, the captain tells his story. There is a mystery-man on board, a passenger of undisclosed identity. He has his hunch and speaks his mind. This stranger holds the answer to their crisis. But who could prove it? 'Why not cast lots?' someone suggests. It seems a risk and rather childish, but all are desperate and the captain yields. The straws are drawn. It is the custom. A paltry way to trace the culprit? A blind surrender, it would seem, to blinder fate. Yet in their case, the Lord transcends their superstition. He holds the lot at His disposing. Who can escape Him? It falls on Jonah and the cause is clear.

A sense of outrage rises now. The incident recalls the patriarch's lie. 'She is my sister,' Pharaoh learns, and soon he calls her to his palace. But ere the adulterous deed is done, God's plagues descend. Unwittingly, he all but sins. 'And what is this that thou hast done to me?' he remonstrates and well he might. The years slip by and Isaac, far from learning from his father's lapse, repeats the dastardly pretence to prince Abimelech. Again the Gentile cries, 'And what is this that thou hast done?' They are dumbfounded, that those who know the one true God, should scorn the truth. And think of David, loved of God, yet rashly numbering his people. It brought down wrath and mass destruction. 'And why,' says Joab, quite nonplussed, 'doth my lord the king delight in this thing?' It was preposterous. Though Pharaoh's faith was less than Abram's; Abimelech's than Isaac's; and Joab's than David's, God still spoke through them to His own. The sinner sometimes says the word that pricks the conscience of the saint. 'What meanest thou, O sleeper?' the heathen captain cries. The attitude of Jonah floors him. Such nonchalance is naked sin. 'Because of you,' Paul writes to Israel, 'God's name is (still) blasphemed amongst the Gentiles.' As Jacob said to Simeon and Levi, 'Ye have troubled me, to make me stink among the inhabitants of the land.' And some of us who bear Christ's Name, do just the same, through disobeying God's commands and disregarding human need.

The crew were fighting for the lives of all; coping with the canvas; dispersing the cargo; securing the hatches. They were running, shouting, heaving, working, doing everything they could to save the vessel. Yet the only man who had the answer was lying fast asleep! It beggared human comprehension. It did so then and does so still.

Our world was never nearer shipwreck than today. The national leaders, faced with the tide and tumult of our times, ride to disaster. Chart and compass, routes and radar, all are gone. No longer do the stars of heaven shine. The voyage proceeds without direction. The unimagined trends have caught us and the current quickens. All strata of society are alerted. Men organise, they mobilise, they march, they riot, they demonstrate; they sabotage and overturn. No effort is too great; no price too high. In time, in substance, life and limb they spend themselves; they fight to death to 'save' the world from wreck and ruin! It is the last mad bid to keep our culture and society afloat.

But what of the Christians and their churches? Still fast asleep and out of sight? Still unaware the storm has struck? We hide and snore while tempests roar; and when men wake us, fail to act. We fume and fumble. Lifeboats dangle. The truth we hold, we do not speak. But Jonah knows his life is forfeit. He sees that only through his death, these men on board can hope to live.

And so the world screams daily in our ears. The ship is stricken. We sluggards of the faith must wake and be expended. Too long our flight from God has lasted. The Master's messages demand that those who bear them die the death. There is no other way to serve; no other way to turn from 'Destination Tarshish' to 'Operation Nineveh.' If we are fellow travellers 'with them', how can we ever hope to 'save them'? In our abandonment, the storm is stilled; in going 'overboard', our destiny secured.

Awake or perish is the summons! Whilst Sisera slept, the tent-pin pierced his temples. As Samson dozed, his locks were severed and his strength destroyed. King Saul asleep, lost both his 'kilt' and honour; and as their eyelids closed, disciples all but missed their vision of the Lord. Whilst workers slept, the tares were sown; and virgins too, were unprepared to meet the Bridegroom. Sleeping for sorrow, friends Peter, James and John knew not the traitor and the Cross were close at hand; And Eutychus, 'sunk down in sleep', falls from his window to death's door. In such events, nought but God's grace delivers. What loss we sleeping saints incur! What dangers slumbering souls invite!

Only the Christ could sleep, when wind and wave were raging. 'Master, we perish!' they whimpered. 'Dost Thou not care?' How small their faith when He, Himself, was calm. If I induce disturbance, I dare not sleep, but when He sleeps, no storm on earth should daunt me. His peace enough for me.

And so the cry rings out inside the ship's dark hold. 'What meanest thou, O sleeper?' With apostolic power its echo shatters our indifference. 'Awake! Awake!' cries Paul. 'Wake thou that sleepest! Walk not as fools! Redeem the time! The days are evil!'[1] The final tempest howls about us. Mankind sinks swiftly to his fate. The plunge is near. Then shall the surge of God's eternities claim all the tragic wrecks of time.

Meanwhile they press him for an answer, 'Tell us we pray thee, why this evil? Tell us we pray thee, for whose cause?'

[1] See Ephesians 5 v. 14–16.

CHAPTER 8

THE PASSENGER'S IDENTITY

The setting is extraordinary. It is a court at sea. Everyone is wet and unnerved. The boat creaks still more ominously; and the whine of the wind grows increasingly vindictive. The water runs coldly back and forth, even in the captain's quarters. There is no time and the passenger is suspect. Now they confront him. Each one is a judge, yet each a prisoner. If they err as judges, they will be sentenced as prisoners. It is a macabre trial. The interrogation begins. The offence is unknown and the offender not certain. But what of the 'lot'? Is such witness authentic? Was God its disposer? But no-one will answer. How the ship shudders! its tremors are ghastly. The wind is indicting. The moments are fleeting. God's voice must be heard.

They see no future. The present is dominant. The sun is darkened. Time is no longer. They must proceed. 'Tell us,' they ask, pleadingly. 'Tell us,' they ask accusingly, 'for whose cause this evil is upon us! Let the innocent be judge, lest all be guilty. Answer us! O answer us! You, who are suspect!' Jonah awakens now. He is caught in the vortex. Their procedure is primitive; but he will not dispute it. He is silent, condemned by a higher court than theirs. As judged by the Judge of all, he will judge himself and no-one else. The nemesis of pagan minds does not confuse him. He knows with whom he has to do. He has sown the wind and the whirlwind consumes him.

'What is your occupation?' they ask. Ah, yes, what was it? Pharaoh once raised this with the brethren of Joseph, to which they replied, 'Thy servants are shepherds, both we and our fathers.' Would God he could say, 'I am a shepherd in Israel!' Had Jehovah a flock in a Ninevite fold? What was he doing out here on the deep? Nursing a grievance? And could that be all? Maintaining his principles? But what were his principles? He looked at these men, so rugged and frightened. And must they all die? Is that what he wanted? A disquieting compassion arose in his heart.

'And where do you come from?' they said, still pursuing him. He thought for a moment – but 'Gath-Hepher' was useless. Were he going to Nineveh, he could have stated his origin. A man sent from God. That's what he should have been ... There was nothing behind him. There was nowhere before him. Just the waves all around him. He had written his epitaph. A man lost at sea.

'And what is your country?' 'And who are your people?' The questions were valid; and he once might have witnessed; but the names sounded empty and despoiled of their power. 'I am a Hebrew.' He would look back to Abram; but he was God's friend and himself like an enemy. Then he confesses, with words that astound them, 'I fear the Lord, the God of heaven,' he explains, 'who made the sea and the dry land.' 'This is the God I fear and this, the One, from whom I flee.'

A kind of logic dawns upon their heathen minds. The storm makes sense. Yet who will allocate the blame? They are dumbfounded. Then someone thinks to ask him, 'Why?' He has deserted. They have harboured him. The Maker of men holds them in mastery. 'O why hast thou done this?' they plaintively ask him. 'Is your mind without reason and your heart without mercy?' But Jonah stands speechless. His creed is now crumbling ... He feels so threadbare in the tempest. A tattered sail that cannot answer to the winds of God. Had he been right, he might have 'ridden it' and trusted God to bring him through, but God, despised, gives men no comfort. 'What shall we do?' they glumly question. 'What shall we do that the sea may be calm . . .?' He hears a panic in their pleading, for 'the sea grew more and more tempestuous'. All hope was dwindling. It is the final inquisition. The court succeeds but hesitates to sentence. It is for Jonah to decide.

The contrast here with Paul is most apparent. At least three kinds of storms are seen in Scripture. There are the Lord's storms such as we have in Jonah's story. This fact gives meaning to the otherwise inscrutable expressions, 'I form the light and create the darkness, I make peace and create evil.' For the purposes of discipline and judgement, the Lord will sometimes bring 'calamity from every side'. It halts us in our tracks to know that God is glorified, not only in the grace that saves but in His wrath that wreaks destruction. Then, too, there are the *devil's storms*. Jesus, Himself encountered one, the day He went to Gadara. The serpent sensed attack was imminent. He thrashed the very lake to fury, but all in vain. Christ broke the demon's grip. The men in chains and tombs go free. Christ's power prevails. Then there are the *natural storms*. That is to say, those storms which arise from the operation of normal physical laws, rather than from supernatural intervention of spiritual beings. To fly in the face of such elemental forces is to court inevitable disaster. The wind Euroclydon, was a known phenomenon. With heavenly light upon this earthly peril, Paul was able to intimate that the voyage, if taken, would incur much harm and loss. In spite of this, the master of the ship preferred to trust his navigational know-how; and he who owned it, because of vested interests, insisted that the ship should sail. Pride in techniques and love of gain remain our biggest liabilities. These men despising God's forewarnings, both in nature and in things revealed, asked only for shipwreck; and the thing they chose, they soon experienced.

It is evident in all this that the case of Paul at sea is

quite different from that of Jonah. Jonah was a disobedient servant; Paul a bondslave of Jesus Christ. Jonah fled from his Master's Presence; Paul says with confidence, 'The Lord stood by me.' Jonah paid his fare as a private passenger. Paul was a prisoner for the sake of the Gospel. Jonah, concerned for no-one, concealed his identity; Paul concerned for everyone boldly witnessed to his Lord. Not one individual could recognise Jonah but the whole ship's company of two hundred and seventy-six souls, came face to face with Paul's Redeemer. Unashamedly he shows his colours. 'I believe God!' he cries. 'I belong to God! I serve God!' Such testimony no storm can drown. It only magnifies its meaning. If once we shirk our Master's business, we soon neglect to own His Name. Life's tumults soon disclose what men we are. Those known in calm will count in crisis. The secret saint cannot deliver. Who fears his fellows, only fails them. In constant silence, our impotence is born.

CHAPTER 9

THE MILLSTONE SINKS

The contrast between Jonah and Paul raises the whole
question of recognition and confession. The word 'identity'
is derived originally from the Latin 'idem', which means
'the same'. Identity and personality are, of course, distinct
ideas. Personality is concerned with what we are in ourselves, be we known or unknown, for quite apart from our
connections, men quickly see the kind of people that we
are. Our social background is irrelevant. Religious or
irreligious, rich or poor, married or single, male or female,
black or white, people of forceful personality soon domin-
ate the scene. Identity, however, defines our links with
other persons, and the things beyond us. It claims a
common factor. It indicates the premise of our category;
that point, where we and others are 'the same'.

The opening words of Jonah's book, established on the
social level the prophet's *personal* identity. Described as
'the son of Amittai', we learn that Jonah and this man
have something in common; something 'the same'. Theirs
is a blood relationship. But on the ship and in the storm,
the weight of crisis forces from Jonah his hitherto concealed vocation. He has a covenant relationship with God
and holds high office from the Lord. This is his *spiritual*
identity. In his predicament, charged as it is with God's
displeasure, he does not tell the waiting crew, 'I am Jonah,
the son of Amittai.' It would elucidate nothing. On the
contrary he says, 'I fear the Lord and have fled from his
Presence', and that explains everything.

These matters affect us more than we realise. When I
was released from the prisons of Red China, my identity

was called in question.[1] Lost for so long to the outside world, changed in physical appearance and deprived of my passport, I had no immediate way of proving who I was, or what my loyalties were. Only after prolonged interviews with the British authorities was my original identity sufficiently attested, to permit of the issue of a new passport as a reliable and bona fide British subject. Identity and personal validity were suddenly of paramount importance in my life. Yet how I longed to be unfettered; to be done with questioning; to be left to myself; to be independent; to exercise my personality in freedom after the deadly repression of the brainwashing. This type of conflict, although so individually expressed, is very prominent to-day.

Man craves, indeed insists upon, the free expression of his personality, yet paradoxically covets the security of a definite identity. Hence the prolification of societies, clubs, associations, sects and orders. Men are gregarious. Like birds of a feather, they flock together, where aims, ideas and goals are shared. Man longs to have at least one thing in common with a section of his fellows. He finds support in 'sameness', though his prime ambition is to gain distinction. Here is his problem. Whilst individuality is prized, and anonymity intolerable to most, to go out on a limb, and that by choice, can sometimes only lead to limbo. To be loved by the crowd, a man must be one of the crowd; yet as one of the crowd, he can be lost in the crowd. If he excels them, he well may lose them, unless, of course, he lives to win them. The natural man is ever anxious to be famous somewhere, but even in the smallest group, not everyone can rise to that; and so today we see an eccentricity that scares us. The hippie hairstyles, haywire morals, things exotic and erotic; these variants baneful and bizarre,

[1] See *When Iron Gates Yield*, the author's account of his three years captivity in Chinese communist hands.

vie without shame for our attention. Each soul would be a part of something, yet each be something in himself. Ferocious loyalty to gangs and parties, goes hand in hand with queerest quirk and crude flamboyance. The uniformity that shelters, soon finds the abnormality it shuns, grotesquely nurtured in its bosom; and whether in the wilder or the milder vein, not one of us escapes these constant contradictions.

If one is different, others join him. A little while and such unorthodox persuasion becomes the fashion and the craze. The immature, flock willy-nilly to identify. A new community emerges, but soon succumbs to stranger notions. The new thing then makes brand-new rebels, and they more different than the different, reach for the stars and gain a myriad fans. This is the way such non-conformity is born. Unfortunately, it fills the world with dwarfs. Although 'of age', we grow more infantile each day.

This process had its rise in Eden. The serpent, Satan, is its source.

The original and true identity of man was given him of God. He does not ask *us* to define it. Its moulding was His own, not something for the creature to achieve. God made man in His image. This was 'the sameness' that he bore. 'I am the Lord,' the Great Creator says, 'that is My Name.' And 'I am He', He unequivocally declares. 'Before Me there was no god formed, nor shall be after Me.' The 'I am He' should rather be translated 'I, the Same'.[2] That is its proper force. Though Persons of the Godhead stand distinct in function, they never act in independence of each other. The Living God, though Father, Son and Holy Ghost, is ever One; each Person still 'The Same'. 'Let *us* make man', God's word decrees, '(and) in our image. Let *us* make man and after *our* likeness and let *them* have dominion . . . over all . . .' Notice the usage of the singular,

[2] See the Hebrew phrasing in the prophecy of Isaiah.

first for 'God' and then for 'man'. See the plural for the human and divine; the 'us' and 'our' and then the 'them'. Now in the singular lies 'personality' and in plurality 'identity'. We may believe 'God is', but in the coming of the Son and then the Spirit, the unknown God becomes identified to faith. We now can know God, personally, and who He is in Person, whereas before we only spoke of His existence. Now all our fellowship is with Him. He is our Father, and we His children. The Son becomes our Saviour, and we His brethren. The Holy Spirit is our Guide, and we His temple. This high identity through God's unmerited bestowing, gives us that true distinction, which makes the angels wonder and the demons quake. His Name is on us, His 'sameness' with us. It gives us consequence in heaven. 'Jesus I know,' says Satan, 'and Paul I know, but who are you?' So Sceva's sons are put to flight as mere nonentities. In Christ alone we grow formidable. God's grace it is, that makes men, men.

Before returning to Jonah we must probe this question one step further. In the beginning, man knew to whom he was related. Stamped with his Maker's image, his freedom lay in using all his gifts to praise the Giver, that is to say, in rendering to his God those things unquestionably His. This sense of true belonging made him a child both safe and glad. He had no personal ends to gain; no private reputation to uphold. Preserving self was no concern. Tomorrow's tasks caused no anxiety. His God was over him. He cared. At rest, mankind could live content and play his destined role within the purposes of God. Yet even so, there was no merging. Whilst in the world, his place was over it. He was not lost in nature nor yet absorbed in God. He shared God's plans beneath the trees. Although one tiny fragment of God's overall regime, he notwithstanding was a person – a participant in rule.

Then came the Fall. The devil taught man to assert

himself; to act as if his links with God were fiction; to play at independence, though all he had, came to him from above. 'But eat the fruit and you'll be godlike!' This was the devil's lure. So Eve and Adam coined their self-styled 'deity', a 'godhood' they could call their own! 'I will be like the Most High,' cried Lucifer. 'And so will I!' man echoed. And in that moment, the tempter and the tempted were 'the same'. So man acquired a 'new' identity. The devil was his father now, not God. The devil's likeness and the devil's works would both be his. He would, like Satan, come to fame through his attainments, influence and power. Owning the 'prince *of* this world', he would be a prince *in* the world. Using his 'independent' personality, he would assert 'the glory' of his 'real' humanity, a glory in its own adherent 'right', untrammelled by the rights of God. 'Self-reliance and not dependence' would be his watchword! 'Dominion via submisson is a hoax!' 'Man must be virile, not servile!' 'There is no godhood but man's manhood in a world of men!' Such were the post-Edenic slogans. The millstone sinks us. Down, down to hell we go. Such 'deity' is insupportable. The clay-men crack. The specks of dust, to dust return. The shoulders of the Christ alone can bear the government. He was obedient. His, only then, the right to reign.

We trace the tragic sequel of the 'garden-gods'. Expulsion, corruption and dissolution are the inexorable and swift results. Cain builds his city, the cultural centre for 'his way', and down the years his godless, violent character brands every city man has raised. Nimrod builds Babel to give the ruined race a name. His tower lifts, rocket-like to heaven, a launching pad for ceaseless insurrection. 'I will be king,' thinks Absalom and gives his theme to Adonijah, who dares to say it. So in the dale the pillar rises, a lonely finger pointing to the sky. Each gained their following; each spawned their cults and causes; each gave to men identities that brought them ruin. Like Satan in revolt, they shared his character and craft; their doom, their master and themselves, 'the same'.

But note, how the first name spoken by the Lord from heaven is Abraham, not Adam. Identified by faith in God, he is God's friend. Divorced from Ur and every idol-claim, he trusts in Him, the great El-Shaddai. All others on the earth are aliens, except God's priest Melchizedek. The patriarch is unashamed. He publicly identifies himself with God, and God identifies Himself with Abraham. Thus God is known on earth, through men on earth that know Him. This is eternal life. This is original identity regained, and more. And when this happens, we at last begin to be.

We, therefore, see that human distinction is not attained by egotistical exertion. I do not need to walk out from 'the herd' to form some special group for my support, security and fresh identity, or by this means assert and then perpetuate 'my being'. Difference is the outcome of a relationship, not the product of ambition. In yielding to 'the Same' that One who made me in his image, I shall stand out before the rebels. Once God is in my heart, His life and likeness show men who my Father is. This makes me salt and light. His works, not mine declare me. Born of His Spirit, I am 'a speckled bird'.[3] And though the fledglings of the human nest may peck me, my Father gives me wings and song. This difference is His glory, not the glorifying of myself. Something that His life achieves, not something I have wrought or even aim at grasping. In this is peace, for what I am, I am by grace. And what am I, you ask? I am a bird of His feather. I am a child of His family and a sheep of His pasture. I am a priest in His house and a stone in His temple; I am a branch in His Vine and a limb in His body. This is a spiritual identity, altogether of Him and for Him. The marks of 'The Same'

[3] Jeremiah 12 v. 9.

are through and through me. In this the saints are all alike
and yet each one remains unique. My God-given personality is expressed in the context of a God-given identity.
They are complementary, not contradictory. Once, I believe,
I can both be, and belong, and thus be at rest in all my life
and labour. We are the stars in His crown, one unified,
glittering spectacle to His praise, yet like the stars of
heaven, He calls us each by name.

III

JONAH AND THE GREAT FISH

THE BOOK OF JONAH

And he said unto them, Take me up, and cast me forth into the sea; so shall the sea be calm unto you: for I know that for my sake this great tempest is upon you.

Nevertheless the men rowed hard to bring it to the land; but they could not: for the sea wrought, and was tempestuous against them.

Wherefore they cried unto the LORD, and said We beseech thee, O LORD, we beseech thee, let us not perish for this man's life, and lay not upon us innocent blood: for thou, O LORD, hast done as it pleased thee.

So they took up Jonah, and cast him forth into the sea: and the sea ceased from her raging.

Then the men feared the LORD exceedingly, and offered a sacrifice unto the LORD, and made vows.

Now the LORD had prepared a great fish to swallow up Jonah. And Jonah was in the belly of the fish three days and three nights.

Then Jonah prayed unto the LORD his God out of the fish's belly.

And said, I cried by reason of mine affliction unto the LORD, and he heard me; out of the belly of hell cried I, and thou heardest my voice.

For thou hadst cast me into the deep, in the midst of the seas; and the floods compassed me about: all thy billows and thy waves passed over me.

Then I said, I am cast out of thy sight; yet I will look again towards thy holy temple.

The waters compassed me about, even to the soul: the depth closed me round about, the weeds were wrapped about my head.

I went down to the bottoms of the mountains; the earth with her bars was about me for ever: yet hast thou brought up my life from corruption, O LORD my God.

When my soul fainted within me I remembered the LORD: and my prayer came unto thee, into thine holy temple.

They that observe lying vanities forsake their own mercy.

But I will sacrifice unto thee with the voice of thanksgiving; I will pay that that I have vowed. Salvation is of the LORD.

And the LORD spake unto the fish, and it vomited out Jonah upon the dry land.

CHAPTER 10

BURIED AT SEA

Every eye in the water-logged cabin is fixed on Jonah. The shock-charged seconds seem longer than centuries. They wait and they wonder. But still he is silent. With tension and anger they hang on his verdict. Yet they do not condemn. The court though convened, has failed to adjudicate. They want just to live now. Nothing else matters. They ask not for vengeance; only survival. The cause has been clarified; the culprit located. They mean him no harm and he means them no hurt. If the sea would but quieten, they would land him at Tarshish. They are strongly indignant but not yet vindictive. And if there's no answer, then how will they do? As Jonah stands thinking, he knows he should speak to them. He hears their strained voices. They seem far away from him. He listens and listens, a man in the distance.

But soon a louder thunder stirs him; that voice which none can silence once it speaks. His Lord has judged him. Now he must judge himself. By that unspoken verdict, he must speak. It is the limit of his flight. He stands there in the way of sinners, but dare not take the scorner's seat. He must judge righteously; judge as he hears. And judgement starts, as always, at God's house. Yes, the sword is towards him. He does not demur. Death is the verdict. It comes as a remedy in the face of his tragedy. He is resolved. He stands in the open now. He begins to communicate.

'Cast me forth into the sea!' he cries. 'So shall the sea be calm . . .' They stand aghast. And must they drown him to survive? And if they live, will not his death be with them till they die? The pagan mind has scruples too. This man's a passenger. He bought his ticket. What if he slept? He was not paid to work. And shall they throw him overboard en route, because he fled from God? His crime was spiritual but have they any moral right to execute this man forthwith? This touches God's prerogatives and none on board has sensed their delegation. The reason for the storm was hard to find. The executioner is harder still! If Jonah were the judge and prisoner, why not the hangman too? But this meant suicide. King Saul, Ahithophel and Judas all took their lives but Jonah was no spiritist, nor yet conspirator. He was God's choice for Nineveh. Through death and resurrection, the God of grace would make this man a sign. Could heathen sailors grasp such truths? It was not likely.

The cry is startling. 'There's land ahoy!' the look-out warns. The court disperses at the shout. How far off course, they dare not think! The news is fraught with hopes and fears. All hands return to take the oars. They row with uncontrolled emotion. Till then they strove to save themselves but now they fight to save this stranger. Their lips are moving as they pull. The sound is rhythmic. 'Innocent blood!' 'Innocent blood!' '*Lay* not upon us this innocent blood!' Yet for themselves they also strive. They fear to die and fear a judgement day. The land eludes them. Madly they row. The sweat is pouring from their backs. The hours pass by. Their efforts fail. The seas are mountainous. The crisis deepens. Unless the storm abates, the ship must founder. A few men gather in the cabin, faint from fatigue. Jonah is there; peace in his face; his struggling over. They know not how to handle him. What if this man, at once the prisoner and the judge, has judged himself erroneously. Then they, as executioners, would be partakers of a deed more deadly than the first, if that could be. What if their 'lot' had predisposed the suspect to incur a sense of guilt and make himself a sacrifice? Then he were just and they

were guilty. What if his choice of death were just one
final subterfuge of flight, a last escape to thwart the call of
God? His sin would be more sinful, and they accomplices
in suicide. How would the tempest ever quieten? Would
it not claim them all?

Jonah stands resolute; his eyes are eloquent. They say
with feeling, 'I caused you this hurt, this danger and this
harm. I am to blame. I shunned the Presence of my Lord
and spurned His claims. I know it is for my sake that this
tempest is upon you. There is no other way for me. There
is no other way for you to enter on God's calm, but by
my death, for while I struggle, wrath is rampant. Once
I yield, then all will cease. Now I am ready. See I am
waiting. Come! Cast me forth into the sea, so shall the sea
be calm!'

The men are moved. Suddenly their gods disperse.
There is one God and He is the Lord. They cry, 'Jehovah!'
The Holy Name is on their lips. 'We beseech Thee, O
Lord, we beseech Thee, let us not perish for this man's
life. O lay not upon us innocent blood, for Thou, O Lord,
hast done as it pleased Thee.'

It is the moment. The ship dips low and with one fling,
the man of Zebulun is thrown by supple arms out to the
seething sea. They watch in silence. He does not fight.
The body sinks; drawn under by the rush of water. Yet
even as they watch, the swell subsides. The foam and fury
slacken. The sun breaks through. The wind is gone. Kneel-
ing they worship. Jehovah! He is the God, who made the
sea and the dry land! Together they sacrifice. Each makes
his vow. One man's immersion has brought them salvation. The God of this Jew, is the God of these Gentiles.
The change around them and within them is equally
divine.

They would arrive of course, at Tarshish, depleted of
goods but rich in faith. All had been lost, yet everything

gained. God, through this victory, secured His witness in the east and west. What news of Him would spread through Tarshish markets and the Ninevite streets. God's blessing always flows when someone is content to be submerged. O cast *me* forth into the sea . . . If I will go overboard and Jesus come on board, then even pagans will believe. It all looks forward to the Greater than Jonah for 'as Jonah was three days in the belly of the great fish, so,' says the Christ, 'shall the Son of Man be three days and three nights in the heart of the earth.' When Saul the storm-raiser got that message he met his death-knell too. 'I am crucified with Christ,' he says, 'nevertheless I live yet not I, Christ liveth in me.'

The only sign for our Ninevite world is a man, crucified and risen with Christ; a man in whom self-will is broken and God's will is paramount. There is no other sign. No other hope. No other way. We must be as He is, in this storm-tossed world.

CHAPTER 11

THE SIGN IN THE SHAPING

One afternoon, I stood with some fifty believers of different nationalities on a shaded beach, looking out across the grey waters of the Store Belt, towards the Danish island of Zealand. Together we sang the praises of our Redeemer and listened to the reading of the Word of God in Danish. Then nine of our number stepped forward one by one, into the waves. Amongst those baptised was an elderly lady of at least seventy years of age. Born of nobility, she had been nurtured in culture, yet only in recent years had come to know Christ in a personal way. I looked at her frail figure, then thought again on the cool breeze and uninviting water; but with a strength beyond her own, she strode out into the tide. Before she was baptised, she uttered a few words. Those who could hear her voice above the sound of the breakers, told me afterwards of her testimony. 'God has broken me,' she said. 'Once I thought I could do many things, but now they are nothing and Jesus is everything!' I shall never forget her, as she walked barefooted over the stones and seaweed, to make her great confession.

It was surely in this spirit that Jonah allowed himself to be plunged into the raging sea. The petulance was gone. He did not say it with a grudge and a grouse, 'All right, the game's up. If that's what you want, I suppose I'll have to submit.' He was not just going through the motions of surrender because he could do no other. Whatever may have transpired earlier, he was acting responsibly now, and before his Lord. Jonah had come to an end of himself; and of himself, he fully acknowledged, an end must now be

made. On this account he was ready for death and burial.
The issue of resurrection, he must leave to Him, whose
air he breathed. Jonah had made his nation, his life. They
stood or fell together and the concept had finished him.
Once *things* become our goal, then death is never very far
away. Lifeless ambitions soon suck the blood from living
men. And though our church and nation may not always
correspond with Jonah's Israel, our studies, sport and work
so often do. When once our family, friends and home
are stamped 'our own', they too assume godlike propor-
tions. Such are entrustments, not our investments. God's
gifts are never goals. They are His means, not ends. His
rich endowments must not merge with our achievements,
else were His glory blurred. All that He has, He proffers
us in Christ, yet we are not the owners but the stewards
of the substance and the talents He imparts. This makes
for great simplicity in handling. Love has no ends but her
Beloved. She seeketh not her own. All that my God has
given is but His channel to the world through me. My
part is not to selfishly conserve such gifts of love, but rather
let His love pass on those gifts in all I do. His bread is
sweet but soon turns sour, if once we fail to share His
bounty. We are but lepers lately blessed. Good tidings are
the hallmark of our day. As fed and glad, we dare not
lounge and sleep. A starving world still waits God's fullness. So Jonah falls, a victim of his own delusion. He sought
to live, but held back life. Now he must die. It is the sole
solution. And must I also go? Yes, without question! The
great immersion claims us all.

Such is the making of the sign. Our Lord refers to it
at least three times. In Luke He speaks of Jonah as a sign
in his person;[1] in Matthew as a sign in his experience;[2]
and later in the same Gospel, as a sign both singular
and final.[3] From these authoritative references to Jonah

---

[1] Luke 11 v. 30.   [2] Matthew 12 v. 39–40.   [3] Matthew 16 v. 4.

by our Lord Himself, we need never doubt the historicity of this little book that bears his name. Throughout Scripture, God's Truth is both stated and illustrated, but when we come to those passages in the New Testament, which attribute a specific spiritual significance to Old Testament persons and situations, then we have what are termed 'authentic types'. Jonah is one of these, and consequently provides us with particular approaches to the meditation of his life and ministry. First of all we can view Jonah *historically*. That is to say, we can consider him, just as he is, in the particular context of his times, tracing the development of his character and the influence he wielded, as he lived and laboured, those many years before Christ came. Then we can think of him *dispensationally*, that is to say, as indicative of Israel and God's dealings with her. For Jonah's impact on the Gentiles depicts quite graphically the course of Israel's destined history and her relation to the nations of the earth. Then we may think of him *typically*, that is to say, how in a limited but definite way he foreshadowed the death, the burial and the resurrection of Christ. Whichever way we view him, however, the truth discerned must be applied *personally*. We need to find out how Jonah and his many adventures impinge on us today. It will already be evident, that the general tenor of this present study, deals more with that which is historical and personal, but as we enter the maw of the fish, the dispensational and typical teaching become more prominent. It would be well, therefore, ere we make our descent to this more sombre region, to get established in our minds the Biblical meaning of the word 'sign'.

There are three Greek words translated in this way in the New Testament and all occur, at least once, in the writings of Luke. His first word 'enneuō' means 'to nod' or 'to beckon', and has to do with the relatives making 'signs' to Zacharias regarding the naming of his son.

Earlier when he 'beckoned' to the people in the temple-court, the word employed is very similar, 'dianeuō'. Then in The Acts of the Apostles, Paul and his escort sailed from Malta in a ship whose sign was 'Castor and Pollux'. No doubt this was a flag bearing the constellation of 'The Gemini' and indicated the ship's registration or ownership. The Greek word here is 'parasēmos'. Thus in the first word we have the thought of 'communication', and in the second the idea of 'identification'. The third word Luke uses is 'semeion'. It is found frequently in the New Testament and whilst containing the force of the first two words goes further to convey the sense of 'authentication'. This is clearly seen when it is translated as 'token' in Paul's second letter to the Thessalonians. There we find this sentence, 'The salutation of Paul with mine own hand, which is the *token* in every epistle.'

The Jews asked Jesus for 'a sign from heaven', yet all his works of power were signs, that is 'semeion', as John makes clear. The things He did, identified Him, and as a result, revealed to those who heard Him, the very One who sent Him. The Father in Him did the works, and was manifested through them. They were thus an authentication of Christ's divine Sonship and mission, and consequently 'signs' in the fullest sense of the term. He also used the same word when He spoke of the 'signs of the times'. The 'semeion', whether in heaven above or on earth beneath, implies an act, which quite explicitly communicates a message. What is done is important; but what is conveyed is more important. It is a deed speaking louder than words. It brings not only blessing or warning to its observer, but responsibility to its recipient. It tells us afresh that when God does something, He always says something. He abhors and always has done, the idle word and idle deed.

Strangely enough, the kiss of Judas is called a 'semeion'.

Although an integral part of his feckless betrayal, it can still help us to understand its meaning. This deed of Judas conveyed a fact beyond the act of kissing, a fact that kissing would generally deny. This illustrates the double-cross, which is the 'semeion' of Satan. When God performs a sign for men, that seen on the physical level points to something richer, deeper and infinitely more wonderful on the spiritual level. On the contrary, when Satan fabricates a sign, the symbol blinds and stumbles the simple, whilst simultaneously hinting to darker minds, the very opposite of what it normally portrays. Thus Satan, himself, the vilest of the vile, transforms himself into an angel of light. His bitter pills are sweetly coated. His bondage masquerades as freedom. He kisses whom he hates. His tokens of affection are his signals to destroy. But Jonah is a sign from God. By reason of his great ordeal, he bears upon his very person the marks of total judgement, and yet concurrently, gives hope of mercy in his strange survival. He is a monument to God's grace and power; an evidence to Nineveh of the goodness and severity of God. The man becomes the message. He is himself, his word; Jonah at last God's sign, God's voice!

This is precisely how our Lord Jesus speaks of him. He refers to him, in two distinct, yet related phrases. He talks of 'the sign of Jonah' and then of 'the preaching of Jonah'. First the man and his moulding; then the man and his ministry. It is only the man upon whom God has wrought a work that God can use *in* His work. Once a man is made sensible to God, then his message will make sense to men. This is true of every sign He fashions and not a few are found in Scripture. Isaiah could write of himself and his family, 'Behold I and the children whom God hath given me are for signs and wonders in Israel.' The man devoted to his God and subject to His discipline, should be a sign to his age, not only in himself, but in the order of his house.

The Lord says to Ezekiel, 'I have set thee for a sign unto the house of Israel.' In all our comings, and our goings, our down-sittings and uprisings, we must be saying to our contemporaries, as Ezekiel did, 'I am your sign, like as I have done so shall it be . . .' And as for John the Baptist, he was the truest signpost of them all. Men heard him speak and followed Jesus. He did no miracles yet all he said of Christ was true. They did not stop and admire the prophet, they went right on to follow the Lamb. Whilst some men are signs in the grace they enjoy, others are signs in the judgement they receive. Think of the words of Moses, 'And the earth opened her mouth and swallowed up Dathan and Abiram and swallowed them up together with Korah, when that company died, what time the fire devoured two hundred and fifty men; and they became a sign.' Or to quote Ezekiel again, 'Everyone that separateth himself from me and setteth up his idols in his heart . . . I will set my face against that man and will make him a sign.' The Hebrew word for 'swallow' used to describe Jonah's experience, is exactly the same as that used of Korah and his company. Whether we think of the jaws of the earth, or the jaws of the fish; the seismic forces in all their immensity, or a muscular contraction in all its intricacy, each in its time and place serves God, the Maker of signs and the Arbiter of men.

Although we shall be viewing Jonah for the most part in an historical and personal way, we must turn now and view him dispensationally and typically, for these aspects of our study are especially linked with the great fish.

The Hebrew term denotes a 'monster'. Whilst this immense creature may well have been a special creation for the occasion, the word 'prepare', which also occurs in the final chapter in connection with the gourd, the worm and the east wind, carries with it more the thought of 'appointment'. A great deal has been written upholding the integrity of this remarkable narrative but inasmuch as Our Lord Himself quotes it as history, it is superfluous to marshal all the harrowing stories in which men have been extracted alive from the abdomen of whales. Perhaps, as some provocatively suggest, we have missed the point completely! Can it be that the miracle is not so much the keeping of Jonah alive in the fish, but rather the resurrection of Jonah after his death in the sea and burial in the fish, to be a living witness to the God who holds the breath of all men in His hand. Think again of that word, '*As* Jonah was three days and three nights in the whale's belly; *so* shall the Son of Man be three days and three nights in the heart of the earth.' The key words 'as' and 'so' may refer, of course, more to the duration *of* the experience than the condition *in* the experience, but the assertion is that in some quite particular way the circumstances of Jonah and the Greater than Jonah are analogous. If the fish is Jonah's tomb and portends 'the heart of the earth', that is to say, the tomb of Our Saviour, it is perhaps not altogether unreasonable to say that just as Christ was physically dead yet spiritually conscious those three days and nights, so Jonah was physically dead but spiritually conscious too. Having sought to escape bodily from his Lord and avoid a direct confrontation with Jehovah, could it not be that Jonah's body was laid aside and his spirit made to answer before the Lord from whom he fled? It may be contended that this precludes Christ as the firstborn from amongst the dead, but this is not so. Christ rose to die no more by virtue of His unstained manhood. All other resurrected persons, although enjoying lengthened days, came surely to their graves at last. The tomb of Jonah still exists and can be visited at Moshed, Zebulun.

The content of the prophet's prayer does lend some weight to these more unconventional suggestions. Consider for instance his words, 'Out of the *belly* of *Sheol* cried I, and Thou heardest my voice.' This is a different word from that used for the 'belly' of the fish. The former means 'stomach' and the latter 'the bowels'. That a distinction is drawn is surely significant. The fish was the physical location of his body but Sheol refers to the spiritual location of his soul. Then he says, 'The waters compassed me about; *even to the soul'*, a phrase which in other parts of Scripture is indicative of death. Finally he says, 'yet hast Thou brought up my life from *corruption'*, which for mode of expression bares striking resemblance to David's prophetic utterance concerning the death and resurrection of Christ. Peter establishes the import of these terms when he quotes it on the Day of Pentecost. 'Thou wilt not leave my soul in *Sheol* neither wilt Thou suffer thine Holy One to see *corruption.'*[4]

Having said this, however, we should perhaps assert that strong though the case may be for such an interpretation, Jonah's experience is essentially illustrative. What Jonah endured is not, in actual fact, what Christ endured. Jonah and his circumstances are an historical and authentic type, but as a type, they still only partially portray the great realities to which they point. We should, however, remember that the intention of the story is not so much to prove that God can keep a man alive inside a whale (something he is well able to do), but that God is the God who can raise a man, even from death, and make him live to Himself. Only that man who stands on the resurrection side of the grave and the heavenward side of judgement, can speak God's message to an adulterous generation. Jonah was brought into the place and power of death in the fish. Whether he actually died or not, is perhaps, not a matter for dogmatism, providing the main burden of the message is kept to the fore and not lost in quibblings of 'science falsely so called'. Whatever the case may be, we are faced

4 See Psalm 16.

here with a miracle that sets forth the wonder of that pre-
eminently greater miracle, the death and resurrection of
Jesus Christ. The sign of Jonah realised in the Saviour is
God's final word to humanity; and that sign realised in the
believer the only witness that avails today.

CHAPTER 12

THE DREAD DEVOURING

Dispensationally, Jonah has to do with Israel and the nations. Typically, Jonah has to do with Our Lord Jesus Christ; whilst historically and personally, Jonah challenges our living in this twentieth century.

The question we first ask when taking a dispensational view of Jonah is, 'Did other prophets have any information regarding the things that befell him and do they give us any ground for applying them to Israel?' Amos, one of Jonah's contemporaries, a shepherd and gatherer of sycamore fruit, prophesying in the south, probably a short while after Jonah's ministry to Nineveh, speaks of Israel in terms that parallel the Jonah narrative. 'Though they hide themselves in the top of Carmel, I will search and take them out thence; and though they be hid from my sight in the bottom of the sea, thence will I command the serpent, and he shall bite them . . . He that calleth for the waters of the sea and poureth them upon the face of the earth; the Lord is His Name.' Then we have Jeremiah, who prophesied much later than Jonah and who witnessed such 'beasts' as Nebuchadnezzar rise rapaciously from the sea of the nations. He describes the experience of Israel in these striking words, 'The King of Babylon hath devoured me, he hath crushed me, he hath swallowed me up like a dragon, he hath filled his belly with my delicates, he hath cast me out.' And again when speaking of the captivity he laments, 'The Lord was an enemy; He hath swallowed up Israel . . . All thine enemies have opened their mouth against thee; they say, we have swallowed her up; certainly this is the day that we looked for . . . The Lord hath done

that which He devised; He hath fulfilled His word . . .'
Ezekiel, priest and prophet of the captivity, writes in a
similar vein. He says, 'they have made you desolate and
swallowed you up on every side . . .' It is hard to believe
that all such references are merely coincidental. Whilst
insisting that the Gentiles were largely responsible for their
own atrocities against Israel, the Scriptures also reveal that
these hostile nations were 'prepared' of God as instruments
to afflict His people in their transgression and apostasy.
These contrasting aspects are portrayed in the 'prepared
fish' of Jonah's story. On the one hand the very nature of
the fish was to devour and yet it was a creature ordained of
God to fulfil that function at a particular place and time.
It foraged after its own appetites, yet fulfilled God's
appointments.

Taking an overall view of history, we can summarise the
dispensational content of Jonah as follows: Jonah was a disobedient prophet and as such, represented a disobedient
Israel. Swallowed by the fish, Jonah is seen outside the
proper function of his calling and under the judgement of
God. In the same way, Israel, who constantly transgressed
the commandments of Jehovah, and in the end crucified
her Messiah, learned to her sorrow what it was to be
devoured by the nations. Today, although not permanently
cast away, she still remains set aside from the mainstream
of her destiny under the judicial dealings of God. But just
as Jonah's drastic experience at the hands of God resulted
in the Gentile mariners trusting Jonah's Lord, so the present setting aside of Israel and her devouring by the nations,
has resulted in individual Gentiles finding salvation in that
very One whose Word she despised. But the end of the
story is not yet. Just as the fish at the sovereign command of
God spued out Jonah, so will the nations in God's appointed time spue out Israel. Reborn as a nation, and seeking
her own will no more, she will eventually execute the

mission originally entrusted to her. In Jonah's restoration, the Gentiles were visited on a national scale, so Israel's recovery in the last days, shall not only be life from the dead for her, but life abundant for the nations worldwide. The key to this dispensational interpretation of Jonah is, of course, found in chapters nine to eleven of Paul's epistle to the Romans, a passage that should be read more often than it is, in conjunction with these Old Testament Scriptures.

We now come to view Jonah typically. The dispensational ground is certainly sacred and fills us with wonder, but when we enter on the sphere of Christ's sufferings as typically portrayed in this ancient record, we must bow our faces to the earth.

In the experience of Jonah, we muse on the baptism of the Lord Jesus, and by that is meant His incomparable 'immersion' of the Cross. For those who will receive it, we have here the Master's steps into the fathomless horrors of Golgotha. It is His way to the Father; yet a way that leads through the jaws of death and down to the bowels of the earth. He goes to that throne where never man sat but via a sepulchre where never man lay. With clean hands and a pure heart he ascends the hill of the Lord; yet as made sin He walks the valley of the shadow and the caverns of Hades. Such is His baptism, enacted in symbol at Jordan and realised in history at Calvary. The waters must cover Him. The grave yawns before Him. Its fangs close upon Him; yet death itself is swallowed up in victory. His matchless dying foils the grave, which all our dyings could not fill. He breaks the seal! The stone removes! His piercèd feet stand conqueror on the accursèd ground. He bore the shame but joy awaits Him. Forth from the deep He comes and through all heaven He passes. Jesus is Victor! Christ the Greater, and the Greatest, fulfils the prophet's lonely cry. 'Cast me forth into the sea, so shall the sea be calm . . .'

Phrase by phrase we trace His footsteps. The prayer-filled
pathos probes our hearts:

'I cried by reason of mine affliction unto the Lord
And He heard me;
Out of the belly of Sheol cried I,
And Thou heardest my voice.

For Thou hadst cast me into the deep,
In the midst of the seas
And the floods compassed me about.
All Thy billows and Thy waves passed over me.

Then I said, I am cast out of Thy sight
Yet will I look again toward Thy holy temple.
The waters compassed me about, even to the soul:
The depth closed me round about
The weeds were wrapped about my head.

I went down to the bottom of the mountains;
The earth with her bars was about me for ever:
Yet hast Thou brought up my life from corruption
O Lord, my God.

When my soul fainted within me
I remembered the Lord:
And my prayer came in unto Thee,
Into Thine holy temple.

They that observe lying vanities forsake their own
    mercy.
But I will sacrifice unto Thee with the voice of
    thanksgiving;
I will pay that that I have vowed
Salvation is of the Lord.'[1]

[1] From Jonah 2.

CHAPTER 13

THE LIVING TOMB

With these words[1] ringing in our hearts we come then to consider their devotional exposition in the typical form:

> 'I cried by reason of mine affliction
> unto the Lord and He heard me.' (v. 2)

The word for affliction is 'straitness' and recalls our Lord's expression, 'I have a baptism to be baptised with and how am I straightened till it be accomplished.' He is not cornered in pursuit like Jonah, but narrowed in the clear-cut line of true obedience. This first cry tells us *how He felt*, although He swiftly adds, 'He heard me.' Wholly entombed, His Father's ear was still wide open to His cry. Though for our sakes forsaken, and for mankind made sin, His holy character, quite unimpaired, holds good before the gaze of God. His Father hears! Then comes the second cry, this time concerning *where He was*.

> 'Out of the belly of Sheol cried I
> and Thou heardest my voice.' (v. 2)

If from beneath the altar the cry of martyr-souls is heard,[2] how much the more, the cry of Him through whom all prayers prevail. This was His constant portion in the way. 'I knew,' He says, 'Thou hearest me always.' He was heard at the tomb of Lazarus. He was heard in Gethsemane, heard from the Hill and heard from the grave. In all the phases of His passion He was heard. With tears and agony His piety succeeds, but listen to His cries. What groanings in the garden, what anguish there beneath the trees, what exercise before the face of God! 'Father,' He

[1] Jonah 2 v. 2–9.   [2] Revelation 6 v. 9–10.

prays, 'if it be possible let this cup pass from me, nevertheless not my will but Thine be done.' The will is *good*. 'Father,' He prays again, 'if this cup pass not from me, except I drink it, Thy will be done.' The will is *acceptable*. Then lastly, to the clank of steel, 'The cup which my Father hath given me, shall I not drink it?' The will is *perfect*.[3] He has proved it in prayer and will prove it in obedience. Perfect it is and perfectly to be performed. So to the Hill He moves. 'Father forgive,' He pleads, 'they know not what they do.' Then when the work is done, there is the end-committal, 'Father into Thy hands I commend my Spirit.' Forsaken judicially, He is still heard paternally. And even though they seal the grave, from the 'belly of Sheol' His voice ascends. Jesus in death is speaking still and better things than Abel's blood. His peerless worth is felt in hell; His character, acclaimed in heaven. His sighs as sufferer soon will cease.[4] His heavenly song shall soon begin.[5] Heard in His life and heard in death, His voice must yet be heard on high. 'In the midst of the church,' He declares, 'will I sing praise unto Thee.'

'For Thou hast cast me into the deep, in the midst
of the seas; and the floods compassed me about.' (v. 3)

These words unfold the three dimensions of His dying; 'the deep', 'the seas', 'the floods'. *'The deep'* itself, depicts that downward tow of all that 'lieth under'; death in its hidden haunts of dark despair, drawing its helpless victims to an unseen world of liquid shade, where dust returns to dust and sediment of men encrusts the ocean beds of time. Thus would it claim Him, yet finds no claim it can exert until our sins are laid upon Him, nor even then can take His precious substance and reduce it. The deep which troubles men and drowns each human generation finds itself a-tremble now. *'The seas'* are death encircling, one

[3] Romans 12 v. 2.   [4] Hebrews 5 v. 7.   [5] Hebrews 2 v. 12.

broad extent of angry sea. It is the thing about us, not only
that which drags us under; an environment as well as a
predicament. And everywhere across its foam-threshed
surface we see a myriad death-throes, as the millions die.
Yet like His birth, His death remains unique. It is the
Father's plunging. '*Thou*' He says, 'hadst cast Me into the
deep.' So from the broad expanse to the vast abyss. It is
God's act. 'It pleased the Lord to bruise Him,' writes
Isaiah. 'The Lord hath put Him to grief. The Lord hath
laid on Him the iniquity of us all.' Cast into the deep to
die, the seascape of a lost humanity sweeps over Him. '*The
floods*', says the Scripture, encompassed Him. This last
dimension shows us the rising tide. It has to do with
heaven's wrath. Moved from above, this tide relentless
mounts on earth. Witness His foreordained submergence.
He dies alone yet dies for all. The deaths of all our human
years surround His head; the sins and griefs of all our sad
millennia become His own. In one vast surge the wrath
which all our ills engender, flows unrestrained across His
head. The Christ is gone, and darkness broods upon the
Christless world. Out of the depths His Spirit cries:

> 'All Thy billows and Thy waves
> passed over me.' (v. 3)

The echo of His voice reverberates through all the Scriptures; from lowest depths to highest heights. 'Deep calleth
to deep at the noise of Thy waterspouts . . . Thou hast
afflicted me with all Thy waves. Thy fierce wrath goeth
over me; Thy floods overflow me.' Yet this is not a drowning man fighting for air. This is the Greater than Jonah
cast by Another into the deep, laying down His life of Himself in submission to death and judgement, that we for ever
might know God's heavenly calm. The place called Calvary
was a place where two seas met. Human malice and divine
wrath comprised that seething cauldron. By wicked hands

God's Son was crucified and slain, yet from eternity the wrath had been determined. The Son of Man went as it was written. 'The billows,' He says, 'are *Thy* billows,' a word which describes the breaking surf. 'The waves,' He says, 'are *Thy* waves' the word denotes the hidden swell. 'I am the man,' He weeps, 'that hath seen affliction by the rod of His wrath.' It is with God alone He has to do. Such were the sufferings of Christ in that dark hour when He was plunged into 'the deep', in the midst of 'the seas' and 'the floods' compassed Him about. Such were the evident terrors of the surf and the unseen terrors of the swell; such the visible and the invisible sufferings of Christ in that day when the sun refused to shine.

'Then I said, I am cast out of Thy sight.' (v. 4)

It is one thing to be cast into the ocean, which here, in all its parts is indicative of death and judgement, but to be cast out of God's sight involves something even more terrible. It means to be forsaken. Although God's ear had heard, His eyes were now averted. The Christ is sinless, but once made sin for us, God views Him in this crucial hour, 'beyond the reach of promise'. With all our sin upon Him there, no claim on God can count, till every claim of law is met. '*Then*' I said – and this was His moment – 'I am cast out of Thy sight.' It marks the acme of His agony; the nadir of His whole emotion. To bear another's punishment is a legal matter, but to lose Another's Presence, is a personal matter. In love, the innocent will endure all things for the guilty, but to lose one's closest contact in the act, must be the hardest thing of all. As 'cast into the midst of the seas', He was cut off from humanity, but once He was 'cast out of God's sight', He was severed, as a man, from the Almighty. We feel the hurt when friends ignore us. What must it be when God forsakes? Surely, the doctrine of Gehenna is expounded in the groanings of Golgotha?

The concept of 'drowning' is used much in Scripture to elucidate divine judgement and righteous retribution. 'Foolish and hurtful lusts,' we are told, 'drown men in destruction and perdition.' We read also how 'the old world perished by water' and that 'the pride of Egypt was covered by the waves of the sea'. Our Lord speaks, too, of a millstone for the offender and his casting into the deep. Yet all such waves and billows Jesus bore. For our transgressions was He wounded and for our sins He died. His were the ocean depths of wrath that stayed our plunge to the Lake of Fire. Now we can bear God's sight because of Him who knew its loss. We stand in white before His Throne, children of song and splendour, filled with His praise. Yet in His great forsaking, hope springs within Him. It will not die. This One who hoped from the womb, hopes still from the tomb. And so He speaks once more in faith,

'Yet will I look again towards Thy holy temple.' (v. 4)

His vision fills, not with the temple made with hands, but with the sanctuary His God has pitched. He looks from things on earth to things in heaven. The Suffering-Servant, co-equal, though He be with God, endures the agony as man. He does not marshal legions from the sky. He rests in God alone, the only One who can deliver; and by such trusting, breaks the bounds of desolation. His innocence is genuine. With confidence He waits the final vindication. The Judge of all the earth, He must do right; so now beneath the maelstrom of God's wrath, He dares to look for heaven and home. All joy is there. With that in view He finds the strength to tread down shame and go right through to God's right hand.

CHAPTER 14

BACK ON THE BEACH

As we move through these heart-rending utterances from within the great fish, we see a certain sequence emerging. We are not allowed to view this spectacle dispassionately. Suffering always has to do with someone, somewhere. Too often we think of 'sufferers' as a subject for discussion rather than objects of compassion; as a mere category of persons, rather than particular individuals. In the opening sentences of this prayer, the one who prays exhibits not only a deep emotion but a clear sense of location coupled with a particular remembrance of those events which have so recently befallen him. It is now a first-person story and we are invited, not just to be observers, but to get beside him where he is. We are expected to step right into the bowels of this nightmare creature. This may seem appalling but it affects us for good; for if Jonah in the fish typifies Christ in His crucifixion and burial, we must remember that we ourselves are crucified and buried with Him too. We are, as the Scripture says, 'baptised into His death'. So the more I appreciate what happened to Christ, the more will I understand what happened to me and be spurred to experience with Him the power of His resurrection.

By means of this prayer we see that Our Lord was plunged into the deep, not merely by men but by God. We have sensed His impact with the water's face, and the heaving seas rising to receive Him. We have pondered the breaking surf and deeper swell surging to engulf Him. Then we came to the point of submergence. We glimpsed that last look heavenward, and saw the swirling waters

cover His holy head. Now in verse five we follow Him
further. We trace His descent, down through the eerie unknown world of death to its unplumbed depths.

> 'The waters compassed me about,'
> He cries, 'even to the soul: the depth
> closed me round about, the weeds
> were wrapped about my head.' (v. 5)

There is something of terror in these words, 'encompassed', 'enclosed', 'enwrapped'. We feel the growing pressure of the water, as that which at first had been an encircling waste, becomes now a deathly shroud. The ragged
breakers flow together and seam it up like a giant zip-
fastener. The sheath is sealed. Enclosure is complete. It is
in this context that the words, 'even to the soul', take on
their fateful meaning. The rush of water not only blurs
the eyes, fades out the hearing and cuts off the breath but
begins to take over the lungs and the inward parts of the
victim. This is an occupation and the soul must go. 'The
waters flowed over mine head,' says Jeremiah. 'I am cut
off. I called upon Thy Name out of the low dungeon.' 'The
waters of death compassed me,' says David. 'Save me, O
God, for the waters are come into my soul.' It is the
moment of expiry; the moment when all the powers of
death, long held at bay, surge like a legion of invaders
across the frontiers of consciousness, to fill man's whole
domain. Such is 'departure'. Yet just as Israel passing
through the seas defeated the Egyptians and left them dead
on the sea shore, so Christ, as He passed through the deep,
achieved by His very exodus, the spoiling of principalities
and powers.

But what of 'the weeds'? This word, the Hebrew 'suph',
is rarely used in Scripture, though here and there, translated 'flags'. The little creel that cradled Moses, was set
amongst the river 'suph'. Out of those waters which

drowned so many infant boys, Moses was 'drawn', the
stamp of death and resurrection upon him for ever. The
weed is emblematic of the curse.[1] It was a weed that circled
Jonah's head; for his rebellion was an accursèd thing. A
weed once circled Jesus' head, for He, the sinless One,
endured the curse for us.

Darker and darker the depths become. Cut off from God,
He drinks the gall of God's anathema. Comfort is absent.
Judgement insistent.

No wonder He says:

> 'I went down to the bottom of the mountains;
> the earth with her bars was about me for ever.' (v. 6)

If Jonah went deep, then Christ went deeper. If Jonah
went down to the bottoms of the mountains, Christ
descended to the lower parts of the earth. Greater in
Person, He is greater in suffering. The word for 'bottom'
means 'extremity'. The descent of Christ could be no lower.
He fathomed the fathomless, and met sin's consequence at
its last dark frontiers. He tasted death to its limits and
tasted it for every man. There is nothing in death or
judgement He has not borne. In all its vast extent and
utmost extremity, our Lord has answered it. There is no
area in the vast abyss left unexplored. He holds the keys
of death and hades. He brought them up from the bottom
of the mountains, from the heart of the earth, from the
depths of the seas. Her bars were strong. The stone and seal
were sure, but Jesus conquered. 'Death could not keep its
prey. He tore the bars away! Jesus my Lord!' Corruption
is powerless. His life is the life of God, brought vibrant
from the dead. He can say and say exultantly:

> 'Yet hast thou brought up my life
> from corruption, O Lord my God.' (v. 6)

[1] Genesis 3 v. 17-19.

With Jonah in the fish, the hope of resurrection grows. Memories of weakness lead on to God's goodness.

> 'When my soul fainted in me
> I remembered the Lord,' he says,
> 'And my prayer came in unto Thee,
> Into thine holy temple.' (v. 7)

As for the mariners, they were idolaters. They had no answer in the tempest nor yet had Jonah while he clung to lifeless prejudice. The empty rituals of mere religionists, whether orthodox or pagan, are alike perversions. He openly acknowledges they have no saving quality. The words he uses are unequivocal. For 'they that observe lying vanities,' says the Scripture, 'forsake their own mercy.'

Jesus saw it at the Cross. There stood the priests and the Pharisees, bound by delusion, esteeming Him stricken and afflicted of God. There sat the soldiers with their dice amongst the dying, gambling for His robe yet without a thought of death. There hung a thief, riddled with bitterness, casting the same in the Saviour's teeth. How close at hand their mercy, and yet how vilely cast away! But now comes the contrast:

> 'But I will sacrifice unto Thee with
> the voice of thanksgiving
> I will pay that, that I have vowed.' (v. 9)

Some have said that Christ could have returned to heaven at any stage of His ministry. This, though morally true, was never vocationally valid. He had put His hand 'Lord, here am I, send me,' and confessed to His Father, to the plough and must go on to the end. Had He not said, 'Thy vows are upon me O God'? How boldly He had spoken, 'A body hast Thou prepared me,' and how gladly made profession, 'Lo, I come to do Thy will, O God.' He had committed Himself, irrevocably. He had opened His

mouth and would not go back. 'I must walk,' He says, 'today and tomorrow . . . The third day I shall be perfected.'
'I must work the works of Him that sent Me while it is day.'
This was the accepted yoke. He must finish the work God
had given Him to do . . . He must needs go through . . .
He could not stay. 'The Son of Man must suffer.' 'There
must of necessity be the death of the testator.' There could
be no tent on the mountain before the Cross on the hill.
First the suffering, then the glory. To this give all the
prophets witness. All through His pilgrimage He says it,
and all through His passion. 'I will pay that, that I have
vowed.' In this intent, He goes singing to the garden and
steadfast to the tree. It was with thanks He broke the bread,
though sold for silver. The Son of Man is glorified, He
says, and God is glorified in Him. So to the Cross He moves.
He is ready for the altar. He will sacrifice with the voice
of thanksgiving. 'I will pay . . .' This is His great avowal.
Such were the tears and song of Jesus on the eve of Calvary.
Now His saints are singing as He wipes their tears away.

Thus He commits His spirit to Him who judges righteously. His perfect love permits no fear. All, all is well. God
will not fail Him. 'Into Thy hands' He says. It is enough.

'Salvation is of the Lord.' (v. 9)

'And the Lord spake unto the fish, and it vomited out
Jonah upon the dry land.' The words of Jesus yield their
meaning. 'As Jonah was . . . so shall the Son of Man be . . .'
'And . . . there was a great earthquake,' we read, 'for the
angel of the Lord descended from heaven, and came and
rolled back the stone from the door, and sat upon it.' 'He is
not here,' he answers. 'He is risen as He said.' Out of the
sea of sorrows we are suddenly come to the land. There is
a man on the shore, in resurrection light. The Greater than
Jonah is here.

IV

JONAH AND THE GREAT CITY

THE BOOK OF JONAH

Chapter 3 v. 1–10

And the word of the LORD came unto Jonah the second time, saying,

Arise, go unto Nineveh, that great city, and preach unto it the preaching that I bid thee.

So Jonah arose, and went unto Nineveh, according to the word of the LORD. Now Nineveh was an exceeding great city of three days' journey.

And Jonah began to enter into the city a day's journey, and he cried, and said, Yet forty days, and Nineveh shall be overthrown.

So the people of Nineveh believed God, and proclaimed a fast, and put on sackcloth, from the greatest of them even to the least of them.

For word came unto the king of Nineveh, and he arose from his throne, and he laid his robe from him, and covered him with sackcloth, and sat in ashes.

And he caused it to be proclaimed and published through Nineveh by the decree of the king and his nobles, saying, Let neither man nor beast, herd nor flock, taste any thing: let them not feed, nor drink water:

But let man and beast be covered with sackcloth, and cry mightily unto God: yea, let them turn every one from his evil way, and from the violence that is in their hands.

Who can tell if God will turn and repent, and turn away from his fierce anger, that we perish not?

And God saw their works, that they turned from their evil way; and God repented of the evil, that he had said that he would do unto them; and he did it not.

CHAPTER 15

THE SECOND TIME

Jonah stood alone on the beach. The wind was silent, the air was still and the sea like a mill pond. It was a day of flawless sunshine. All was so calm, and the song, *Salvation is of the Lord*, was still singing in his heart. He was a man wholly changed.

When leaving Gath-Hepher, he had had money in hand but now he had nothing. He had paid the fare, though he offered no prayer. Headstrong and determined, he had set sail for Tarshish; a passenger not a sailor; a man in his own right, 'entitled' to his own convictions; going where he wanted to go. He had felt tired, of course, but in good health. As a highly respected 'minister of religion', he had stood by the establishment. It was a pity the rank and file were so ignorant and that God Himself sometimes did not agree with him, but as the spiritual leader of his day and the prophet of the hour, he had known what he was talking about. How self-assured he had been. It seemed like a by-gone era, though only days ago.

Now he stands on the beach, a solitary figure in the sun-light, his long thin shadow pointing back to the deep. Out from the shallows he staggers, where the fish had disgorged him. The water in little rivulets, trickles coldly down his cramped bare limbs. His last vestige of clothing clings like a limpet to his back. He is alive but exhausted. The stench of the vomit still lingers about him. He walks a few steps forward. The tiny waves ripple in, along the endless coast. He reaches beyond them to the dunes. He feels the warm dry sand push up through his toes. His eyes glance uneasily downwards. His skin is scarred and discoloured, an unearthly white from his great ordeal. He would never be the same again, yet somehow it did not worry him. He was perplexed but could not feel dismayed. All he could do was stand in the silence and bask his wasted body in the light. There was nothing to say; at least not audibly. He could only be glad; and only be thankful. Then came that far-away feeling, but he did not fight it. The tempest was past. The conflict was over. He was strangely content and his peace was deepening, a peace as yet he could not understand. Then out of the stillness and the empty shore, came the voice of his Lord. Like a stirring in the sand and grasses, he could hear its ceaseless whisper:

'Arise, go to Nineveh, that great city;
And preach to it the preaching that I bid thee.'

That was all.

It took him back to Zebulun and his own beloved hills, to that breathless first encounter, ere the great wind sought him or the fish devoured. He was in the Land again; and communing with his God again. Once he had been strong but then he would not go for Him. Now he was so weak yet willing to obey. This was the second time; the final and the only time. God's wrath and mercy filled his eyes. The marks of death stared from his face, and yet he lived. He felt his dereliction; yet sensed renewed vocation. God's choice remained. This spectacle, grotesque, but blessed; this spued-up jetsam from the tide; this ugly fragment of a broken man, judged, killed, yet raised again, would serve as God's sole vessel in the earth to meet the hour. By weakness such as this, God fells the mighty. God wields the things that are not, to humble things that are. His apex-eye discerns. His will decrees. No other man but this shall preach His word in Nineveh. This is His sign. The hour has struck. The anger falls! 'Rise, go!' He says. The man submits. God's great imperative succeeds! His grace prevails!

The drama takes on magnitude. God's operational triangle moves to fulfilment. We sense relief when Jonah chooses to obey. We also have our moments when silence will not prove an answer. God speaks again and we must act. Such crises are not easily resolved. The clear-cut 'Yes' cuts us to pieces. No ear so deaf as that which will not hear. Elihu says, 'God speaketh once, yea twice and man perceives it not.' When God reiterates, shall we prevaricate? Through His persistence, our resistence comes to light. The 'second time' can break or make us. It shows the seriousness of God and tests the fickleness of man. That the dream was doubled unto Pharaoh twice, says Joseph, 'is because the thing is established by God'. 'And the Lord was angry,' says the Bible, of Solomon, 'because his heart was turned from the Lord God of Israel who had appeared unto him twice.' By reason of 'the second time', God brings blurred men to focus. 'At the second time,' says Scripture, 'Joseph was made known to his brethren'; and when the cock crowed twice, the heart of Peter was disclosed. The second time is grace extended; but if ignored is judgement sealed. Paul's writings would uphold the concept. 'A man that is a heretic,' he writes, 'after the first and second admonition, reject' — a principle of discipline, laid down by Jesus. Yet to the man who does respond, a striking testimony is given. Like David he can say, 'God hath spoken once, twice have I heard this, that power belongeth unto God.' For some, our story has a special meaning . . .

I have known, perhaps in some degree, what it is to stand on the beach, the shadow of the man I was, disgorged by a 'monster' on the sands of time. God who spoke to the fish, spoke also for me. The three long years in the communists' maw were like those three long days and nights . . . but then the moment came. They could not hold me any more. Surely I had cried by reason of my affliction unto the Lord and he had heard me out of the belly of hell.

I could sing *Salvation is of the Lord*. After my release I came to Hong Kong. Soon the excitement died away and I began to realise, like many before me, I would never be the same again. Something had happened. The marks of a great ordeal were upon me and what could I do? In the August of 1954, some nine months later, I sat in a little room at The Park School, Yeovil. I was there for a young people's missionary conference but felt so weak, I could hardly speak. One day in the quietness, I read of Paul's defence before the Hebrew people. He told of his conversion in the way, and how the holy Ananias helped him in the days of his bewilderment. 'The God of our fathers,' he said, 'hath chosen thee, that thou shouldest know His will, and see that Just One and shouldest hear the voice of His mouth.' The words were wonderful but hardly moved me, then suddenly I read, For thou shalt be His witness unto all men of what thou hast seen and heard. And now why tarriest thou . . . ? This sentence to me was not only the Word of God, it was a word *from* God. Not only something He said to Paul, long, long ago, but something He was saying to me. In my youth He had told me so clearly, to preach Him to the nations, but I had hardly begun, though I went to the ends of the earth. Now was the second time. In spite of everything, there was no cancellation of His call. Like a stirring in the sand and grasses, I too had heard His whisper in my heart. It is from such a place He bids us rise and go to Nineveh. It is in brokenness His fullness comes. When strength is gone and nothing can be done, He shows us once again our task. He makes the utterly impossible, our business. Then faith begins and mountains move. All else is vanity.

God's voice goes out to many, yet still He calls us one by one, and each by name. To some their name is doubly spoken. They shine like stars. 'Abraham, Abraham,' sounds the cry. He witnesses to resurrection. 'Samuel, Samuel,' calls the Lord; a prophet, priest and judge emerges. 'Martha, Martha,' Jesus says. She owns Him as the Son of God. Then 'Simon, Simon,' Jesus warns. The weeks go by; the Spirit fills; he speaks with power. 'Saul, Saul,' the voice from heaven rings and Jesus saves. How happy then are those who hear their names so called. We hear it once. We hear it twice. We should with utmost urgency obey. We need not doubt the brief He gives. His words are clear.

'Go unto my country and to my kindred,' is the word to Eliezer.

'Go speak to Pharaoh,' is the word to Moses.

'Go in this thy might, have not I sent thee?' is the word to Gideon.

'Go tell this people,' is the word to Isaiah.

'Go to the lost sheep of the house of Israel,' says Jesus first.

'Go home and tell thy friends,' He says in Gadara.

'Go quickly to the streets and lanes . . . and bring in . . . the poor, the halt, the maimed and blind.'

'Go tell His disciples,' says the Angel.

'Go . . . into all the world and preach the Gospel,' is the final mandate of them all.

There is a call we share with all believers. That has to do with salvation. But there is a call to each believer which has to do with service. The initial 'Come', issues in the subsequent 'Go'. And when He says it the second time, our second 'No' is quite precluded. We face an order from the Throne.

And so it was that Jonah rose and went to Nineveh, not only to preach the word of the Lord, but to preach it *according* to the word of the Lord. Submitted to it he could now declare it. God's work performed God's way, is God effectively proclaimed.

CHAPTER 16

CITY OF BLOOD

Nineveh lay like a sparkling jewel beneath the azure splendour of the brightening sky. As yet few stirred in her streets, though here and there could be seen a work-worn peasant trundling his cart of vegetables to the open market. Down by the riverside, the water-carriers were at their labour, dipping their tubs into the quiet flowing waters, hoisting the yoke to their shoulders, and then mounting steadily, the broad stone steps to the upper pavement. In the arcades, a few small traders were already on the move, taking down their shutters and arranging their wares in the cool of the day. Beneath the shadowy arches and at the street corners in the poorer districts, food-vendors stood, kindling their charcoal and boiling their oil in hope of early customers. The silent hours were breaking into action. The air was filled with a growing whisper, the twittering of a myriad birds perched on the ledges white with droppings. Soon a cock's crow joined their chorus and from the shrines of the city, there softly sounded the sluggish drone of priestly liturgies. This was dawn in the orient, that peaceful moment when dreams of night still hold in check the fears of day; when stately buildings stand ethereal, and tapering towers are seen as artists' fingers on a canvas sky. It is the time between, when all is beauty, and nothing hints of haunts where things are sinister and vile.

Yet as the sun shines brighter, there is a shadow deepening. Those fortress walls that guard the Tigris, glower darkly down upon its glassy face. Their gaze is pitiless. Apart from echoes of command as each watch changes, they keep their silence. The cries behind the cheerless gates are muffled and unheard. The people pose no questions. The stones which know the answers, do not speak. Disposal of the 'enemies of state' is not for asking; nor is it practical to feed emaciated slaves who serve no more. There is no problem. Efficiently, the thousands come and go and Nineveh grows great. It is not hard to disappear. The river is its life and death. No stench of blood need rise. Men are expendable; the perfumes of Arabia not far away.

Socially, the imperial capital was a city of contrasts. Class-awareness was strong amongst the people and those of like profession tended to congregate in certain sectors and stamp them with their own peculiar character. There were districts of scribes, of clerks and priests. Whole urban areas were dominated by craftsmen plying certain skills, such as the bakers, the weavers, the joiners, the sculptors or workers in various metals. In other parts lived the money lenders, the civil servants and the officials, whose elegant and cultured homes bespoke their personal wealth and status. This natural segregation of society upheld the interests of the monarchy, enabling them to handle industry, levy taxes and cunningly manipulate one class against another, without a needless show of power. The currying of favour was a national pastime. The system bred its diplomats and middlemen, a cult of wily go-betweens. Bribery and corruption abounded. Blackmail and extortion were the order of the day. In such a social structure, guilds and fraternities fought for a hearing at the seats of power. As champions of their class, they could exact conformity in rule and practice from the groups they served. Whichever way a plebeian turned, the horns of some dilemma thrust him through. His overlords drank up their gains in instant revelry. The stakes were high and risks were great. The morrow held its own uncertainties. To thwart the set-up hailed disaster. Avarice distorted standards. Ambition staged its dark intrigues. Purging by perjury usurped the law. Professional killers stalked the streets. To liquidate as well as legislate became the function of the crown. 'A city of blood' they called her; and she had earned her name.

This sick society, although divided, formed one immense hierarchal pyramid. The king as topstone, crowned its pinnacle. His royal sceptre lent coherence. The families round the throne were therefore few, their place and privilege held directly at his pleasure. From this élite emerged the satraps, governors and priests, the generals and the ministers of state. A deadly nepotism gripped all the echelons of power. The emperor's word was law and they upheld it. The weapons of coercion were their might. Whom he disdained they slew and whom he would they kept alive. Yet not in force and wealth alone his power lay, but in his links with 'deity'. In Nineveh's antiquity, the name of Asshur stands illustrious.[1] He was the founder of their culture. First, their inaugural city, and then the nation, bore his name. This hero-figure was their god, the 'god of empire', the high embodiment of all their military achievement. The king, as head of state, enshrined and wielded Asshur's power. To doubt the king, was viewed as calling 'god' in question. To slander Asshur's regent was affrontery to 'god' himself. The pagan mind did not rebel. Such concepts of authority, which stretched beyond their monarch to 'a man divine' gave them security. It was a grand delusion. The untold might of Nineveh proclaimed it 'real'.

Along with Asshur,[1] Nabu, their god of wisdom, and Ishtar,[2] the goddess of love, enjoyed the veneration of the

---

[1] 'Nisroch', an Assyrian deity mentioned in II Kings 19 v. 37 and Isaiah 37 v. 38, is thought to be another designation of 'Asshur'. It is described by Philo as having an eagle's head and a human form. It was in the temple of Nisroch that Sennacherib was assassinated in 698 BC. But see Genesis 10 v. 11.

[2] It is interesting in view of Jonah's experience, to learn that the Hebrew, 'Nineweh' is a translation of the Assyrian 'Ninua', which, in turn, is a rendering of the earlier Sumerian 'Nina'. This was a name of the goddess

people. They held chief place amongst their deities. The king, as Asshur's choice, was thus not only head of state but at the centre of the state belief. He shared the reverence of the gods they served. An inner circle of magicians were ever ready with their counsel. The mediums, astrologers and priests became the chief advisers of the realm. In such a scene of villainy, debauchery and folly, the blind led on the blind to certain judgement.

Their literature, already two millennia old, grew with the years to an unrivalled fame. The countless tablets scored with complex cuneiform, were stacked and filed. Such records held a history that looked back to the flood. They told of laws, of medicine, and court proceedings. They covered contracts and transactions. Their teaching linked with earlier Hammurabi, that King of Babylonia, whose moral code was once renowned. Yet notwithstanding, all their skills merged hopelessly with base desire. The arts and industry lived by atrocity. The passion to acquire, was married to the passion to indulge. The more refined their culture was, the crueller their techniques became. It was aesthetic savagery, a place where beauty served the beast. The horror of the race was with them. The more their men 'developed', the more they must devour.[3]

The likeness of Assyria to our present-day regimes need

Ishtar, written with a sign depicting a fish inside a womb. Whilst there is no reason to link this symbol with Jonah, yet his arrival from the 'belly of the great fish' may have startled the pagan mind more than we realise and raised hopes of a love that could ultimately pardon the repentant. The planet Venus was also identified with this goddess.

[3] For instance, in D. D. Luckenbill's *Ancient Records of Assyria and Babylon* (Anc. Records Ser. 1) we read the following translation of a document from the reign of Ashurnasirpal II, 884–859 BC:

'I built a pillar over against his city and I flayed all the chiefs who had revolted, and covered the pillar with their skin. Some I walled up within the pillar, some I impaled upon the pillar on stakes, and others I bound to stakes round about the pillar . . . And cut the limbs of the officers, of the royal officers who had rebelled . . .

'Many captives from among them I burned with fire, and many I took as living captives. From some I cut off their noses, their ears and their fingers;

not be laboured. Hitler, Stalin, Mussolini, along with Castro, Mao and Nkrumah, would look with relish on such 'strength of rule'. The affinity is great. Nor is this fanciful, for excavation makes it clear that Ninevite society held much in common with the social 'vision' of 'Il duce'. Yet all these modern counterparts have, like their kind so long ago, just 'forty' days to live. There is a time-clock set in lustful power. Its final demise is determined. The voice of Jonah still comes thundering down the years. The sword on high hangs by a thread. The Living God still writes His verdict on our walls. And though His thunderbolts may linger, we sense the moral cancer in us all. The measure of our sin marks out the limits of survival. And when like Sodom and Gomorrah, this little world goes down in flames, we still must answer in the Judgement. God is not mocked. The times of Noah were steeped in violence. So were the times of Nineveh. Yet in these past decades, more men have died a violent death than all the blood-stained past can muster. The tares of ruin grow and ripen. The sand runs low within the glass. Our days are numbered. 'Repent or perish,' says the Christ. The sign of Jonah is our need, Christ, crucified and risen! The God who kills and makes alive, our only hope and only fear!

The 'sergeant' watched with some impatience. They were too late. The day had dawned. The sun was up. 'Get moving!' he goaded and the bodies slipped more swiftly to the water. He watched emotionless, as each in turn swirled weirdly downward and away, through all the dark

---

of many I put out the eyes. I made one pillar of the living and another of heads, and I bound their heads to tree trunks round about the city. Their young men and maidens I burned in the fire.

'Twenty men I captured alive and I immured them in the wall of his palace . . .

'The rest of their warriors I consumed with thirst in the desert of the Euphrates . . .'

translucence. Drop-outs they were, from yesterday, and most were dead. But some still lived. They looked like drowning kittens in a pail. They struggled briefly; then were gone. 'How many now?' he snapped. 'Just ninety-nine,' the 'corporal' said, as if he counted sheep. 'Make it the hundred,' came the grunt. 'Who cares? It's only for the record.' And with that comment in their ears, his men marched back to breakfast.

It must have been the Tigris, we immediately presume. But why not rivers nearer home, the Volga, Tiber or the Elbe? Why not the Yangtze now, or Father Thames to-morrow? There are but forty days to live?

So to the hour. The man from Zebulun had come to Nineveh.

Who came from God.

CHAPTER 17

THE TERROR OF GOD

Jonah found the land of Assyria a broad undulating country. To the far north rose the precipitous mountains of Urartu, and to the east, the Zagros ranges of Media. As he approached the Tigris valley, the dry terrain was cut across by numerous streams, and dusty roads began to cleave the maze of irrigated fields. Each hour the scene was changing. The nomad lands receded. Oases, kraals and bedouin camps lay lost amongst the dunes. The trek along the desert routes reached to its goal. The furnace-heat and chill night bivouacs would soon be but a memory. Emerging from the glaring sand, the fresh green vegetables relaxed his eyes. The roadside thronged with peasants selling melons, dates and citrus fruits. The laden carts and chariots increased and all the time the sky-line filled with age-long Nineveh. This was the world metropolis; the fabled heart of highest civilisation. Such walled immensity dwarfed all his prior imaginings. 'Arise and go to Nineveh,' his Lord had said; and even He had called it 'great'. The phrase seemed so ironical. 'A city of God', is the full translation. It was the old superlative the Hebrews used, when human norms appeared exceeded. Its choice was surely not haphazard. Did it not promise hopes of grace? Long centuries later, when Paul, the apostle, preached in Corinth, his Lord who sent him to that den, told him quite plainly, 'I have much people in this city.' Such is the marvel of God's mercy. He sees the sinner as the saint to be, and in the foulest heathen race, claims an inheritance for Christ, His Son. In the purpose of God, this 'city of blood' would be a 'city of God'. Where sin abounded, grace would much

more abound; and the God of the Jews, be God of the
Gentiles also!

The following morning Jonah stood on the west bank of
the Tigris and looked away to the farther side, where the
city in all its magnificence lay mirrored in the river, whose
waters barely seemed to move. Now there was only the
crossing before him, and in less than an hour he would start
on his mission. He did not brood. There was no sermon to
prepare. The man was not divided from his message, and
God, Himself, had made all preparations. He stood, not in
the role of some extempore informant. His single thrust
was a 'kerugma', a God-sent preaching from the Throne.
His proclamation was prescribed. He was no longer free.
One sentence in the Assyrian tongue,[1] no more, no less, his
Lord had given. He spoke as heralds speak, not by some
personal whim. He proffered news, not vain opinion. As
sent from God, he preached the preaching he was bidden.
Was it five words he had to say? His piscine scars and
mottled skin made him authentic. With understanding he
would teach, not with some 'tongue', unknown to him or
them. As one thrown overboard, he saw vast Nineveh, all
overthrown. This was his strength. The man, himself, gave
import to the words he spoke.

The tiny craft drew in to where the worn stone steps
rose up to greet the water-gate. He had arrived and now
must act. To walk the full perimeter, he knew, would
prove a three days' journey, though one brief day might

---

[1] The Assyrian language was almost certainly a form of Aramaic (see
Isaiah 36 v. 11 and II Kings 18 v. 26) and substantially the same as Chaldee.
Ninevite inscriptions of weights and business contracts were, by the 8th
century BC, being written in Aramaic, and it was used extensively for
commerce and diplomacy. The Assyrian language therefore, may not have
been altogether unfamiliar to Jonah. There is little doubt he would be
acquainted with the Syrian form of Aramaic, being born and bred in an
area liable to Syrian invasion. It is interesting to note that Daniel 2 v. 46 to
7 v. 28; Ezra 4 v. 8 to 6 v. 18; 7 v. 12–16, and also Genesis 31 v. 47 and
Jeremiah 10 v. 11 are all basically written in Aramaic and that all the
Semitic words quoted in the New Testament are in that language.

H

see him through.[2] This was not Jericho; nor he, an army.
He came not with the priestly trumpets, but rather with
prophetic fire. No scabbard hung about his waist. The
Spirit's sword was quite unsheathed. He came not to surround and then subdue, but with the Word of God to
sever; in one clean cut, to strike that central blow, to
utterly expose the soul and spirit, the thoughts and intents
of their hearts . . .

Think on him now. The walls rise heavily in stone above
him. His meagre form is lost amidst the crowds that throng
the arch. He walks some yards in deepest shadow, then out
he steps, into the brilliant light. His loneliness is quite
appalling. Would we have spoken? Though so incongruous
upon that pagan street, the Hebrew 'fragment' is not silent.
The centuries yield no other moment quite like this. He
stands the sole trustee of saving truth amongst a million
Gentile souls; the rustic prophet from Gath-Hepher, holds
God's own answer to their need. This time he will not fail,
nor will he sleep. His voice is thunderous. It storms their
hearts a thousand times, until they shudder at its force. The
voice of many waters fills it, the voice of Jahweh, powerful
majestic, clear; the voice of Him who breaks the cedars;
that voice which marks out sin with tongues of flame. It is
the Lord, who with His still small voice, speaks in the
conscience when the storm has ceased. That voice that
brings His Presence near, almost inaudible but deafening.
That voice incessant and insistent. That voice which will
not be denied; the voice of God Almighty in the soul!
Jonah had known it. Jonah could preach it. What man
among them could resist it?

'Yet forty days . . .' he cries, 'and Nineveh is *overthrown*!'
'Yet forty days . . .' he cries again, and people turn to

[2] This was probably the period of time taken to encircle the entire urban
area of Nineveh with its enclosed pasturelands at the official reckoning of
approximately twenty miles a day. A day's journey into Nineveh, in this
case, would be the time needed to walk from one side to the other.

gaze and wonder. 'And Nineveh,' he warns unflinchingly, 'is *overthrown*!' The climax rings with fearful fervour. The citadel of pride is breached. A terror rises in their breasts. There is no hiding. It is the terror of the Lord.

Just twice elsewhere this word for 'overthrow' is used. We find it in Psalm 41, where God makes smooth the invalid's bed.[3] It has to do with ruffling up a flattened mattress. 'As a palliasse is lifted up, turned in the air and then thrown down, so will I take you,' God is saying, 'so will I somersault you in the air, till shattered, broken and subdued, your vile iniquity is fully judged.' Job also uses it. 'God overturns the mountains by the roots,' he says.[4] And God through Jonah, makes it clear that strong though Nineveh may be, her pyramid of power can be upended and destroyed.

There is no conversation; no dallying to discuss. For more than twenty miles the prophet walks, and hour by hour, the people's grave misgivings grow. He does not halt or cease to cry. God's repetition stabs the heart. His searing sentence cleaves the conscience. The masses shake. Is it the ghastly mien of Jonah's face that strikes such apprehension in their minds? Is there a darkness in the sun? Or comes a whirlwind from the desert? Do deathly tremors shake the earth? Is there a rumour from the skies? Is there a flood-rise on the river? Is this the god-man from the sea? O what a Presence in the breathless air! What sense of terror and of fate! It is the God who overturns; the God of tempest and of storm! The God of Israel in their streets! The Lord from heaven, with whom at last they have to do!

From lip to lip the news is borne. The birds have flown. The rats go forth. With bated breath the people speak. The alleys fill with haunting fears. The day wears on. The beauty of the dawn is gone. They sense the portent of their doom. A deep unease stalks through courtyards and bazaars;

[3] Psalm 41 v. 3.   [4] Job 28 v. 9.

invades the workshops and the crowded marts. It stirs the hovels and the brothels. It masters princes, satraps, whores; it bows the army and the slaves.

'Yet forty days . . .' It is the period of probation. Full forty days the flood prevailed. For forty days and twice at that, Moses lingered on the Mount. For forty years God proved His own, who in the desert failed and fell. For forty days Christ fasted, then strongly put His foe to flight. For forty days He taught His friends, and from their midst went up on high. The Jewish punishment was forty stripes (save one). It is God's period and point of trial. Beyond it, there is no returning. Within it, issues raised must be resolved. Such was the Ninevites' dilemma . . .

The streets are hushed as Jonah's footsteps die. The business wanes. The abacus is still. A messenger attends the royal apartment. The halls are fraught with brittle tension. The curtain parts. An audience is given. The man stands dumb. He trembles at the knees. He knows not what to say, though royalty requires that he should speak. With furtive air he makes report. 'Your majesty,' he says, 'a foreigner with piercing eye, goes preaching through our Nineveh.' Just one dread sentence he proclaims! Some think he came forth from the sea. Yet who can tell? It almost seems the legend lives. I listened at the water-gate. Your majesty, I heard and feared. I saw the panic spread. The people kneel in thousands in our streets, yet not to you, my sovereign liege, nor yet to Asshur. It is The Presence they acknowledge. Such are my tidings. Your subjects wait your counsel from the throne . . . May I withdraw, your majesty?'

The king was obviously displeased at this emotional intrusion. He dealt with 'facts' and with officials; rarely with persons. He found them an embarrassment. If once emotion coloured duty, demotion was not long delayed. Dispassionate, impartial rule, this only could become his sceptre! Yet he was baffled.

'Stand where you are!' he roared impatiently. 'What did he say? This alien fellow in our streets?'

All eyes turned coldly on the quivering runner. The man was broken. He paused, then half-hysterically cried out. 'No more than forty days, my lord, and Nineveh is overthrown!'

The king would normally have cursed him but suddenly grew silent and morose. A deathly stillness gripped the room. Each sound was audible; almost sepulchral. At last the emperor spoke, his startled gaze fixed on his courtiers.

'I hear a noise,' he said. 'Tell me, you ministers of state, what is it?' Then came a voice from those who waited.

'It is the sound, O king, of strong men weeping.'

The king turned white and viewed his hands.

He saw them red like crimson . . .

Who never saw them red before.[5]

---

[5] Adad-nirari III, 810–783 BC, was very likely the king on the throne of Assyria at the time of Jonah's mission to Nineveh. After the great revolt of the rural nobility and certain high officials in 827 BC, Shalmaneser III, 858–824 BC, who is mentioned on the 'Black Obelisk' found by Layard, discredited his older son, the crown prince, and gave the right of succession to his younger son, who became Shamshi-Adad V, 823–811 BC. In five years he crushed the serious insurrection which had spread, in all, to twenty-seven cities. He died, however, whilst his son Adad-nirari was still a boy, and it was only when he had grown to manhood and authority that under his vigorous leadership Assyria regained its former might. Adad-nirari III pursued the policies of his grandfather and succeeded in the further subjugation of Syria, which was Israel's militant northern neighbour. He actually entered Damascus and put Benhadad III to tribute. No doubt, this eroding of Syrian influence over the years, was the chief historical factor that enabled Jeroboam II, under God, to restore the northern frontiers of Israel. One cannot help but wonder whether Adad-nirari III had cognisance of these matters and thus was predisposed to heed Jonah's warning to Nineveh in view of the accuracy of his earlier prophecies concerning Syrio-Israelite relations.

It is just possible, on the other hand, that Jonah arrived at Nineveh in the days of Shamsi-Adad V when the issue of the revolt still hung in the balance or even in the last precarious years of Shalmaneser III. In this case the overthrow of the capital, Nineveh, loomed as a present and distinct possibility. There is little doubt that there were genuine grievances and injustices which sparked off this rebellion, and the repentance and moral change in the king and the whole hierarchy of his ministers of state (Jonah 3 v. 5–7) could well have been a major cause in saving the Ninevite throne at that juncture of its history.

CHAPTER 18

THE DUST AND THE ASHES

The sonorous boom of a copper gong sounds heavily along the highways and the byways of the city. An ominous pause and every ear is waiting. Then, 'Boom!' It goes again. This time the town-crier hails the people. There is an edict from the king. His dirge-like words are like some grave lament that leads a funeral cortège to the tomb. The weight and measured cadence of the royal decree, weds pathos to authority. Yet not to Jonah or the monarch they submit, but rather to the Living God, whose word first bowed their hearts.

> 'Let neither man nor beast, herd nor flock taste anything:
> Let them not feed, nor drink water: but
> Let man and beast be covered with sackcloth and cry mightily to God: yea
> Let them turn every one from his evil way and from the violence that is in their hands.
> Who can tell if God will turn and repent, and turn away from His fierce anger
> That we perish not?'

The old stone steps are empty now. No morning tubs tip in the timeless flow, nor do the female slaves thrash washing in the dawn. No vendors take their stance beside the gates, nor do the rumbling carts grind onward to the central square. No children scamper through the streets. There is no laughter. The beasts of burden idly stand, still tethered in their stalls. The fields are empty; shops are closed; the pageantry has gone from all the palace courts.

The fear of God has silenced all. The wisdom from on high
begins . . .

'So the people of Nineveh believed God . . .
And God saw their works . . .'

The faith that works, that is the faith that saves. First
came the Word. It made them hear God's voice and by that
hearing, faith was born. They had to learn as Jonah did,
'Salvation is of the Lord.' Yet faith's validity is only proved
by actions such belief engenders. God looks for works be-
gotten by the word received; works that bespeak repentance; that tell of truth productive in the inward parts,
truth grasped initially by faith. 'Believe on the Lord Jesus
Christ,' the apostles told the gaoler, 'and thou shalt be
saved . . .' Once he believed, we learn how he washed their
stripes, was willingly baptised and gave them food. His
faith was real. His works declared it. Works could not save,
but none the less they evidenced salvation. No fasting, sackcloth, tears or ashes, in themselves could rescue Nineveh,
but all these showed a change of heart which God acknowledged. Paul's word regarding this is left on record:

'By grace are ye saved through faith;
and that not of yourselves;
it is the gift of God.'[1]

And then again, he shows that,

'Not by works of righteousness which we have done,
but according to His mercy He saved us . . . that
being justified by His grace, we should be
made heirs according to the hope of eternal life.'[2]

He underlines the teaching as the text proceeds.

'This is a faithful saying,' he writes, 'and these things I
will
that thou affirm constantly, that they which have

[1] Ephesians 2 v. 8. The pronoun 'it' refers to 'grace'.   [2] Titus 3 v. 5.

believed in God (note 'belief' is prior), might
be careful to maintain good works.'[3]

The Jonah narrative emphasises the consistency of God's
dealings with mankind throughout all ages. Whatever the
dispensation, justification before God is always by His
grace and through faith, albeit a faith attested by good
works. The sequence of our story makes this abundantly
clear. 'They believed God.' That is, they received not only
a prophet of God but the God of the prophet. In listening
to Jonah, they submitted to the Almighty. In receiving the
sent-one, they accepted the Sender. It reminds us of the
way in which certain people acknowledged John the
Baptist. They heard him speak, then followed Jesus. They
took heed to the herald and went after the King. So the
Ninevites believed God and 'God saw their works'. He
acknowledged the visible outcome of the inner-working of
His revelation. 'Faith' therefore is the parent, 'works' the
child, and God's pure Word the source of each.

Two other incidents are often quoted to explain this
truth. One has to do with Abraham and the other with
Rahab.

In Romans chapter four, we read how Abraham was
justified by faith, yet in James chapter two, we are told he
was justified by works. In comparing the chronology of
these incidents in the patriarch's experience, we find that
his justification by faith distinctly took place, when he
accepted God's promise as to his seed before Isaac was born.
When James, however, asserts that he was justified by
works, we find that this occurred many years later when he
offered up Isaac on the altar. So sure was Abraham of the
earlier promise, that he counted on God to raise his son in
order to fulfil it. Thus his faith was evidenced in his works.
Indeed, it was only because of such faith that he dared to
obey God on the mount. God saw his works and owned his

[3] Titus 3 v. 8.

faith from heaven itself. 'Now I know,' He says, 'because thou hast not withheld . . .'

In Hebrews chapter eleven, we read how Rahab was also saved through faith. 'By faith,' it says, 'Rahab perished not with them that believed not, when she had received the spies with peace.' Yet James, in chapter two of his letter, insists she was justified by works. Once again, however, we must note the timing, for this latter aspect came to pass, when she had not only received the messengers in peace but had sent them out another way. The faith that received them was saving faith, though only God could see it. From the human standpoint, she might have received them to betray them. When, however, she gave them safe passage, the reality of her faith was seen, not only by the spies, but by all Israel. They had assurance through these visible works that she was a justified woman. They knew of a certainty that she had believed.

'So the people of Nineveh believed God and God saw their works.' This is the way God's saving grace unfolds. It originates with Him and is granted to faith. It then operates in its recipients and their works declare it. Justification before God is not something good works obtain, but a God-given relationship, from which good works proceed. Such works are not the beginning of our acceptance but a proof that we are already His. If we trust our 'good works' for salvation, we are saying that we do not need a God to save us. Good works are then our pride and the beginning of our condemnation. When the word of God is received in the heart, then the works of God are manifest in the life. There was no other way for Nineveh and there is no other way for us. By grace we are saved, and that through faith. It is never of ourselves. 'Salvation is of the Lord.'

The sight is strange; indeed, is almost inconceivable. The morning court is over. The guards and counsellors are gone. The throne of jewels, ivory and gold, is vacant now. Maybe its final edict has been given, 'for who can tell,' it said, 'if God will turn . . . ?' And whither has the emperor gone? We trace his way, first to his private suite. The shreds of sackcloth strew the lavish rugs. The royal robes lie rudely on the crumpled bed. He is not there. We wander through the sumptuous rooms but all we hear are muffled cries and groans of men. Down in the lowest courtyard kneel his slaves. Their lord kneels with them. Amidst the many, who can know him? Each bows in sackcloth; each looks the same; each man a sinner in God's sight; each one come short of God's pure glory. There is no difference, says the Scripture; all have sinned; all stand condemned. But God be thanked! Because no difference is asserted, the Lord who is rich unto all who call, has mercy on all who repent and believe. Joel's recent word is powerfully exemplified. 'Whosoever shall call on the Name of the Lord shall be delivered.'[4]

The happenings in Nineveh are more than arresting; they pierce *our* conscience too. In my childhood, when radio was still a wonder, I remember listening on a Saturday evening to the well-known programme, *In Town Tonight*. In a brief half-hour, celebrities in London were brought to the microphone to share their personal experiences with the public. I can recall nothing of what they said, but I do recall the lead-in to the programme. There was the roar and bustle of the London traffic, the changing of gears, and if I remember rightly, an old lady crying, 'Sweet violets!' Suddenly a stentorian voice called through the hubbub, 'Stop!' Then all was silent. It seemed miraculous! How could it happen? It did in Nineveh; and in the life of many a man, has happened since. The Eternal Sentinel accosts us. His crackling 'Halt!' is backed by fire. Rooted we stand, caught out, uncovered and accused. Now

[4] Joel 2 v. 32.

nothing but our sins concerns us. I know it well. Maybe you know it too.

A friend of mine was once confronted. A crude, erratic individual, he scourged his youthful staff with oaths and curses. Then all at once, God's hand was on him. He was arrested by the Unseen Spirit. The man was helpless. He could not shave. He could not sleep nor could he cope with his commitments. Half-crazed with guilt, he sought one friend, and then another. For hours he conversed with his minister, but found no peace. Until one night, a Christian girl spoke simply to him of her Saviour. His heart was touched; he trusted Christ. His sin was purged and fears removed. The staff next morning were astonished. Their boss was changed, nor did they hear him swear again. Once God says, 'Stop!' we must stand still. Another step can mean our ruin.

Three things displayed the Ninevites' repentance; their fasting, sackcloth and their ashes. Each one pronounced a clear-cut 'No!' 'Fasting' said 'No!' to appetite. 'Sackcloth' said 'No!' to appearance; and 'Ashes' said 'No!' to ambition. All that in which they gloried, suddenly became their shame. The things of gain became their loss and everything was forfeit in the light of God.

Repentance always means a 'fasting'; a 'No!' to self, whatever the abstention. The Christ of God 'pleased not Himself'; how much the more we men who love our sinning. All that we have is leased from God. We dare not talk of independence, much less indulgence. He made us each a temple. We make ourselves a den of thieves. He stops our business with His lash. No wonder! It is His kindness; else were our fate His ceaseless flame.

Yes, all repentance has its 'sackcloth'. Clothes are externals. They fortify ephemeral distinctions. They tell our rank, our finance and profession. They may be kingly, priestly or prophetic. Our 'uniform' declares our work.

Sackcloth makes level. It tells of grief, not merely for a sad event but for the sin that makes us vile. Its wearing bears true witness to the bankrupt state; its coarseness brands us crude and rude. It says that what we are beneath God's gaze is crucial. All else is pride.

Yet true repentance goes right through to 'ashes'. 'Dust' was inadequate for Nineveh. It is not mentioned in the story. 'Dust' speaks of death, for dust we are and unto dust return. It tells us of the sinner's end and intimates his well-earned wages. To kneel in dust is to acknowledge what we are without God's breath; that sin, when finished, brings forth death; that men have only once to die, then face their judgement. When in repentance this is seen, we come at last to taste the ashes, for ashes speak of fire, fire that consumes. To repent in dust is to admit, that I who sin must die in Time; but to repent in ashes, that I who sin must burn in Eternity. Should these two symbols break us now their substance will not claim us then. Thus Jesus says, 'Except ye repent, ye shall all likewise perish.' It is the voice of The Greater.

Who then will lay aside his 'royal apparel'? We reign as kings! Will any leave his throne and kneel beside his fellow men? We come to dust, but are we come to ashes? The days run out. Who bows not down, must in the end be overthrown.

We deem this hard, yet in the edict of the humbled king, God's Spirit speaks. It is the wisdom from above, born of God's fear.

First he says 'Stop!' No, not initially from sinning, but rather from the lawful acts of life. Stop eating, drinking, tending cattle! The mundane things of everyday have always blinded men to crisis. It was so when the ark door closed. All things continued as they were. They ate, they drank. They married wives. Then judgement fell. Had they once stopped 'the ordinary', they might have heard 'the extra-ordinary', that is God's sacred word through Noah. So will it be at last, when Christ returns in power. Sleeping and eating, working and drinking, marrying and begetting, today's dark world will come to judgement — the means of living still accepted as the ends of life. He who repents must stop. Stop for reflection, stop for inspection and stop for correction. We cannot kneel in ashes and take our breakfast too!

But he continues, 'Cry! Cry to God; cry mightily!' The word denotes 'strong crying'. It is the 'asking, seeking, knocking' cry, that claims an answer. It means a coming, and involves believing; a trust in God that passionately maintains He is, and will reward all those that seek Him. For all who stop and cry, a hope is born. For all who hasten on, there is a crying yet to be; and who can face it? For Nineveh, God's ear is open. His eyes behold. He sees them trembling, as they grasp His Word, and stoops to save.

The final order of the King is 'Turn!' 'Turn from your evil ways?' That is your own direction and intention. 'Turn from the violence in your hands!' Your deeds in lust and life and lip.

It is the movement of complete repentance. The sudden halt. The turning 'to' and 'turning from'; a Spirit-energised conversion.

Christ's commentary remains disturbing to anyone who thinks today. 'The men of Nineveh,' He says, 'shall rise in judgement with this generation and condemn it, for they repented at the preaching of Jonah and behold, a greater than Jonah is here.' It points us on through all the centuries, on to the End; one moment's fateful history, kept for posterity on the fringe of eternity.

And there I see the Great White Throne and all the faithless of our times. I see the Head once crowned with thorns, the Head of Him who now presides upon that last and terrible Assize. I see the books and they are opened. I sense the silence of the speechless throng. Sun, moon and stars witness against them. All revelation was despised. Memory and conscience point their fingers, vociferous now, who once were stifled. The blood of Christ proclaims the verdict. What once would save must now destroy.

Yet there I see them, there within the emerald rainbow, clad in the whiteness of the Lamb; the Ninevites, whose joy for ever is the Lord of Jonah, the Lord who showed them grace in Time. They do not speak but in their tens of thousands, rise. How eloquent their judgement; so irrefutable, so sure! For them one sentence opened heaven and yet for millions there, The Sign, Himself, was not enough. God is absolved; He gave His Son; the Christ rejector stands condemned.

<h1 style="text-align:center">V</h1>

JONAH AND THE GREAT KINDNESS

THE BOOK OF JONAH

Chapter 4 v. 1–11

But it displeased Jonah exceedingly, and he was very angry.

And he prayed unto the LORD, and said, I pray thee, O LORD, was not this my saying, when I was yet in my country? Therefore I fled before unto Tarshish: for I knew that thou art a gracious God, and merciful, slow to anger, and of great kindness, and repentest thee of the evil.

Therefore now, O LORD, take, I beseech thee, my life from me; for it is better for me to die than to live.

Then said the LORD, Doest thou well to be angry?

So Jonah went out of the city, and sat on the east side of the city, and there made him a booth, and sat under it in the shadow, till he might see what would become of the city.

And the LORD God prepared a gourd, and made it to come up over Jonah, that it might be a shadow over his head, to deliver him from his grief. So Jonah was exceeding glad of the gourd.

But God prepared a worm when the morning rose the next day, and it smote the gourd that it withered.

And it came to pass, when the sun did arise, that God prepared a vehement east wind; and the sun beat upon the head of Jonah, that he fainted, and wished in himself to die, and said, It is better for me to die than to live.

And God said to Jonah, Doest thou well to be angry for the gourd? And he said, I do well to be angry, even unto death.

Then said the LORD, Thou hast had pity on the gourd, for the which thou hast not laboured, neither madest it grow; which came up in a night, and perished in a night:

And should not I spare Nineveh, that great city, wherein are more than sixscore thousand persons that cannot discern between their right hand and their left hand; and also much cattle?

CHAPTER 19

ARROGANT AFTERMATH

Once more the scene is changed. The urban clamour yields
to rural peace. The city is traversed. The open country lies
beyond. With scant concern, the prophet seeks a vantage
point. He is oblivious. To watch its fate but not to share it,
this now his occupation. Just forty days! Not very long for
Nineveh, though all too long for Jonah. The city and the
sign, alike are tested. In argument and action vigorous, he
finds suspense and lull depressive. The multitude is gone.
The solitude reveals his soul. How glad he is and yet how
sad. At first bemused, his thoughts confused hold him in
tension. The spectres of the past revive. The days slip by.
God's sun still shines upon the city. The unjust open to
the light. He might have known. Did he not say when still
in Zebulun?

> 'Yes, Lord, I prayed to Thee,
> This was my saying.
> Did I not tell Thee
> When still in my country?
> That's why I fled from Thee
> And took ship to Tarshish.
> I knew Thou wast gracious
> And a God who was merciful,
> Slow in Thine anger;
> And great in Thy kindness
> Repenting of evil.'

What irony! As God's displeasure relented, Jonah's displeasure fermented. As God's grace and kindness prevailed, Jonah's smallmindedness quailed. We are dismayed

at Jonah's attitude, yet should we be surprised? Moses, the meek, strikes at the rock; David, the psalmist, lies with Bathsheba. Have prophets no passions? The saints themselves are only sinners saved by grace. The earthen vessel, treasure-filled, is far from flawless. Yet one thing cannot be denied; a man of God in sinning, sins more greatly. If knowing right, he does the wrong, more blame accrues. Once character runs high then every fall becomes conspicuous. The sins of those more spiritually mature, are frequently most catastrophic. The stumbling babe can rise again, his babblings pass, but errors in the public man, none will excuse.

How like the Spirit to be gracious! He never makes men superhuman. God's characters are never heroes in the normal sense. In Him alone lies their achievement. All else is flesh and blood. We are not demigods but mostly little fools that godly fear and simple faith make wise. Such moments are too few. They should be longer. God does not wink at Jonah's slur. Note His perspectives. The flight to Tarshish staged rebellion; that must be judged. The present quibble, vaunts opinion; that needs instruction. He does not blast him with a tempest, nor use a whale when one small worm will do. He asks him questions in the sunshine; helps him to analyse his anger; helps him to see its untold danger. A course and not a curse is thus God's answer. The gracious discipline proceeds.

How rage distorts. Its tears are blinding. Yet some will say, 'Was God Himself not wrathful too?' There are two words.[1] God's anger,[2] fierce and fiery, links with His nostrils. It is 'the snort' of righteousness outraged. In Jonah's case the word means 'burning'.[3] A temper smoul-

---

[1] Although the second word is used of God's anger elsewhere in Scripture, in the text of Jonah, the use of these two words, respectively, for God's anger and Jonah's anger is consistent.

[2] Jonah 3 v. 9 and 4 v. 2. Heb. 'aph'.

Jonah 4 v. 1, 4 and 9. Heb. 'charah'.

dered in his heart. To come so far; endure so much; then prove a laughing stock? Yes, he could stand it; but acquiesce in causeless grace, that spared a Nineveh to scourge his people? It was too much. His earlier prejudice returns; it storms his soul and reason bows. But human wrath works not the righteousness of God. It only kills. No gulf is spanned. Old chasms deepen. Once man hot-headed and hot-passioned acts, he must destroy. The anger first recorded in Old Testament times, was Cain's. It slew an Abel. The anger first recorded in New Testament times, was Herod's. It slaughtered infants. Such anger always kills, and kills the innocent. Once 'filled with madness', priests and laymen planned Christ's murder. The Nazarene must go. They first distorted, then devoured. Lust always liquidates. So feud and fire run on. Few kill when cool.

Yet why be angry in this carnal sense? It happens, always, when the 'I' looms large. Its forced expansion makes for friction; asks for protection; expects vindication; then resents all frustration. Judicially the 'I' of Jonah had been dealt with. God's waves and billows had prevailed. He was immersed. The fish was ready. The 'I' was sentenced, dead and buried, a figure of today's baptising, that plants us with the Christ in death. This did not need to be repeated. Its meaning, though, must be exerted. What happened then should mould him now. He knew the facts. He had himself proclaimed them. 'I am cast out of Thy sight.' Those were his words. In view of this his 'I' must now be reckoned dead. Out from the depths he came, raised up to stand in grace, upon that resurrection shore. Old things were gone; fresh works begun. In newness of life he preached to Nineveh, God's yielded man.

But men are straws. They waver in the wind. The prophet and apostle once again show kinship. Simon Bar-jona knew God's grace, but faltered sadly when those Jews from James came in.[4] He lets the mood of Joppa cloud him. The vital lessons fade away. So now with Jonah. Tense and tired, the man explodes; but God is a match for peevish tantrums. He knows His children; and their needs. How 'father-like He tends and spares us.' How 'well our feeble frame He knows'. Jonah, once judged, is judged no more. God chastens now, as sons are chastened. He preached God's chosen word in public. Can he not speak his own in private! Of course he could, if he were still his own, but now he is God's; His sign for all the years to point men on to Calvary. No sign displays its own ideas. It shows the way, else were its meaning void. With patience, God permits the outburst. Jonah will learn. He must become what God would make him, not live again by pride of race. The deep had shown him God's severity. Now he must answer to His goodness. Repentance must be deepened and resentment quietened. We need to tell ourselves again, 'Christ Jesus came into the world to save sinners.' Nor dare we modify the phrase, 'of whom I *am* chief'. See how the present tense is used. Not yesterday's conversion but today's contrition. This is the emphasis. The eternally contrite, are eternally thankful. It is in grateful men, humility matures. Should I revert in thought to what I was, and try to salvage earlier prides, my joy recedes, for then my hope is not in Christ or what His love can do for me but in myself, once judged as hopeless on the tree.

Does he not hear himself expostulate? Is Jonah deaf? Six times the pronoun 'I' occurs, then 'my' three times and 'me' twice over. So recently this man was spiritual. What life and peace: What power, too! Today his carnal mind returns. He longs to die. The gladness of the 'second time' and all its sweet obedience, slips from his heart. The madness of the 'first time' surges in. But God who called, would take away his first reactions, to make the second last for

[4] Galatians 2 v. 11–14.

ever. He would replace the carnal load with all the benefits of grace. Such was the issue. It had been settled in the sea, though Jonah still despised its meaning.

A startling echo fills the heavens! 'I will be like the Most High,' roars Satan. 'I will set my throne above the stars of God.' We each have heard that cry; and most have learned it, at least in some degree. How near the devil is when 'I' expand. It is his spirit that inflates us; his vain audacity that makes us 'big'. 'I told you so!' pouts Jonah to his Lord. What prostitution of communion. He takes the stage. He resurrects his old identity. In loneliness and holiness, he preached in Nineveh. Maybe he came and went unknown, a voice that spoke and died, to leave with men the abiding Word. Not in his own name did he speak but in the Name of Him who sent him. As God's ambassador, he had not failed. Christ called him great and so he was, in this capacity. Why then not leave it there, content to serve and stage no comeback? But he would still be Israel's champion; still argue with their ends in view; still be their Jonah. Yet he pertained to God alone. There was no sharing.

When would the facts sink in? He thought he knew Him.

But Jonah had to think again.

CHAPTER 20

BETTER TO DIE

Jonah's crises, although mysterious, answer clearly to our own. His soul, like ours, is a battlefield! There are spiritual persons behind the visible people. The devil is active, though never once mentioned. Silently he plots intrigue. He stands to lose Nineveh, thus manipulates Jonah. God is on trial. The issue for The Greater than Jonah, is not just the training of a difficult child, but the defeat of the devil, at a seat of his power. Jonah is rocked by the force of combat. As yielding to God, he is clothed with His greatness, but really is minuscule, tumbled and turned in the wind of the moment. His moods change quickly. He can be so imperious but still prove vicarious. At times like the present, he appears quite ridiculous. The apostles are not better than the prophets. Simon Bar-jonah, who is always so similar, exhibits vacillation, too. The men who seek to side with God are bound to know the tides of war. Amongst the twelve, such characters as John and Judas help to give us light on Jonah.

With them, that which is of God and that which is of Satan develops side by side. Both men are brought to focus as the Cross draws near. From the very outset, the ambitions of Judas are obscure. We know nothing of his first contact with Jesus, nor is his real reaction to the Messianic claim divulged. He was hardly a theologian, that much is clear, nor yet a politician. At the most he was a careerist and in the end 'a devil', though Jesus knew him when He chose him. As Bunyan taught – 'those who for lucre, follow Christ, will for the same forsake Him'. Piece by piece, the traitor's aims emerge, and as they do, he takes the stage and

claims the limelight. How prominent his name becomes!
Satan inspires him; Satan indwells him; Satan possesses
him; and phrase by phrase, Satan 'enlarges' him. The
sequence is significant. He mimes an act of feigned benefi-
cence. He bleats like any sheep but nourishes a wolf's
intention. 'The poor are robbed,' he claims. 'Such waste
deprives the underprivileged.' Thus Judas speaks and
Mary's love-gift is discounted. How very much he has to
say! What liberal gestures he displays! How active now!
He is the great philanthropist, yet secret agent too. How
big he is! How able for these dual roles! Judas will do what
none in power can do – place Jesus in the leaders' hands.
One kiss will do it. His simple act, the subtle sign! What
skilled sharp-practice! Just 'thirty pieces' is his charge. A
bargain price! Some middlemen might ask for more. Not
he! The time and terms must come together. The feast
posed dangers. Hard cash, not promises, he wanted. Once
pocketed, the Nazarene would be *their* problem. If Jesus
really stilled the storm, then He could scatter them. How
he would laugh if that should be. If Jesus failed and they
condemned him, why should he worry? Just one more
charlatan would die, that's all. But was that likely? He had
not thought on meekness; that Christ, though able, would
not exercise His might. This was His hour. The Cross was
chosen. To it He moved. Although divine, He calls no
legions from the skies, nor powders Pilate on the Pavement. He does not slay them from the tree but prays
forgiveness on His foes. Such blood is innocent. Judas perceives it all too late. He sold himself when he sold Jesus.
The silver gained will not redeem. 'See thou to that!' the
rulers say. So Satan magnifies, then disembowels. If ever
man attained 'identity', that man was Judas. All history's
treason haunts his name.

But look at John. Of him the very opposite is true. He
rests in Jesus. As one who leaned upon His bosom, he

found an everlasting strength. As one who lay upon His breast, he heard the heart-beats of His love. Christ's power and pulse are real to John. He does not ask for greatness now, though once he did; the near-place, not the high-place, is his joy. Yet how instructive! The nearer to his Lord he gets, the more anonymous this man becomes. Amongst the twelve, he is the one 'whom Jesus loved', though each was loved, yes, even Judas. His links with Christ make him renowned. His closeness intimates his stature. His namesake's cry he makes his own. In later years he writes it down, for 'He must increase,' said the Baptist, 'I must decrease.' Christ is His all. Though socially connected, John calls himself His bondslave. No earthly lineage counts. Born from above, the things above are beckoning. Enough that men should say that he has been with Jesus. He is that 'other disciple'. It is the spirit of the least, whom Christ's makes great. It calls to mind another 'nameless' saint, whose praise was in the Gospel. Such 'are the messengers of the churches,' writes Paul, 'and the glory of Christ.'[1]

Now the name and fame of Jonah were linked with the rise and fall of Nineveh. Events, to him, were now more vital than the Eternal. While Nineveh survived, his future showed no prospects. His past alone held 'glory'. It still restrained him. But what a haze such hankering brought! It veiled his God; think how he spoke to Him. It veiled his fellows; think how he spurned them. It veiled himself; he talked like any fool. Robbed of his own projected image, life lost its meaning. 'It is better for me to die,' he said, 'than to live.' If he had recalled how he *had* died, he would have wanted to live; live to his God, who quickens men to serve. Mere history deludes us and memory tends to puff us up. God resurrects 'dead men' to 'works before ordained'. We strive to resurrect our past, but dead works

[1] II Corinthians 8 v. 18 and 23.

there will never live to God. They only make our 'bigness'
linger beyond the context of our deeds. The 'things behind'
must be forgotten. We must press on. Whom God makes
great, is great indeed and to such greatness, Jonah needed
now to grow. Faith counts on all that God has done and
reaches forward. Milestones assist, not when they tell the
distance covered but when they tell how far to go. As Jonah
loiters, all seems lost. One day with God; the city crumbled.
One day alone, brought him defeat.

Had Jonah thought more on Elijah, he might have been
quite different . . . The glory of Carmel turns to gloom on
Mount Horeb and public victory is eclipsed in personal
depression. The moods of godly men are disconcerting.
How inexplicable they are, but in this case there is a clue.
We read that 'he, himself, went a day's journey into the
wilderness'.[2] The man who walked with God, now walked
alone. The tragic contrast makes it clear. A day with God
on the mountain and he is answered by fire; a day with
himself in the desert and God answers him nothing. What
strength and weakness! Elijah prayed and rainfall ceased.
He prayed again. The torrents fell. Then Jezebel vows
vengeance and fear takes over. Faith has two hands and
clasps its Saviour. Fear has two legs and flees its spectre.
Faith walks in company. Fear goes alone. So went Elijah.
God's power recedes; his time-sense fails; he calls for wrath
and pleads for judgement. His 'facts' are faulty. No fire
descends. For years he sensed divine intention. Now he is
'blind'. Baffled, he cannot wait. He asks to die. Once more
his prayer is not accepted. No grave is found. Heaven's
chariot waits. Elijah, man of flame and sign, had still to
learn. How pot-holed is the way that leads beyond our
Ninevehs and Carmels. The Lord pursues us even when
our work is 'done'. We think we have 'finished', but God
has so much more in hand. 'What doest thou here?' He asks

2 I Kings 19 v. 4.

His servant. Caught in the wrong place and asking the wrong thing, like Jonah, he replies uncouthly. How soon man breaks in isolation. 'Go forth,' he is told, 'and stand upon the mount before the Lord.' He knew that phrase and used it often. It was the premise of his preaching, 'As the Lord liveth before whom I stand . . .' The utterance had made men tremble. In the presence of the Lord his ministry began, and by His living strength it was maintained; but now he huddled in a cave. 'The stand,' his Lord was saying, 'must be renewed.' Only as standing in the presence of God can you stand for God in the presence of men. 'I am Gabriel,' says the angel, 'that stand in the presence of God and am sent to speak unto thee and to show thee these glad tidings.' So spoke the heavenly messenger to Zacharias, the priest. If this was needful for angels, how essential for prophets. No ministry exists apart from its origin. When we speak those things we have seen with our Father, then like our Lord we are marked off from the scribes. Elijah standing before the Lord, could boldly face a man like Ahab, but once he chose to stand alone, he could not stand before a woman. In spite of this, however, it is good to know that the victories of God, whether achieved through Jonah or Elijah, or for that matter anyone else, are not erased by human weakness. The anointing oil is not rescinded but only extended. The mantle cannot be destroyed. It simply passes on.

At times like these man has his 'remedies'; but God has medicine all His own. Coals, cakes and cruses, give their strength. The earthquake, wind and fire subdue. He has His tempest, fish and gourd; His fiery gales and wriggling worms. He feeds us up or files us down and through it all His still small voice accuses. Prophets had passions like our own, and inner problems as they laboured. Like us, 'I' trouble was their chief undoing. They shared the symptoms of the self-same blight. We covet sympathy, and love men's lauding; pine for support and lust for power. We may be coddled, even cudgelled, but in the end all feeds despair. It happens when we walk alone. We may not wilfully desert Him, but such forgetfulness is dangerous. Like Joseph and his Mary, the days go by, and we can think the Son is with us. Sad inadvertence will not spare us. We must return and seek with sorrow, till we have found Him in God's house. All questions Jesus answers there . . .

If self-preoccupation affected only inward mood, then I alone would be disturbed, but moods molest. Ill-humour can inflict its wounds. Once 'I' am on the throne and wield the sceptre, the thought of mercy tends to die. Self-righteousness *will* call for judgement. Each one of us pontificates our whole life through. The world must be put right. Yes, even God! The Pharisee in each of us cries out for 'justice', though men are righted best by love and grace.

Hear what the 'big' one says:

'*I* thank Thee *I* am not as other men are, extortioners, unjust, adulterers, or even as this publican.
I fast twice in the week.
I give tithes of all that I possess.'

And hear what the 'big' son says:

'These many years do *I* serve thee, neither trangressed *I* at any time thy commandment
And yet thou never gavest *me* a kid
That I might make merry with *my* friends.'

Mercy for the publican and pardon for the prodigal? It is unthinkable. They don't deserve it! Forgiveness of such sinners would make sheer nonsense of our 'righteous' record. The 'I' enlarged insists on vengeance. The world is dreadful. Let dissolute humanity be judged and punished. So Jonah argues; yet is it, that God's good may triumph? Would he not find *his* vindication if Nineveh were overthrown? If grace were shown, the Lord would be their all in all; His servant fade.

Jonah is shaken. How can he be the nameless brother? His life-long cause? Was it no more? The shell cracks open; the newly born dare hardly venture. How can he walk? And must he fly? He is bewildered. How can grace reign? His moral background still resists it. This is the end for him and Israel. What can he do? Where can he go? 'It is better for me,' he asserts, 'to die than to live.' To say it once is not enough. He must repeat it. Yet how his words reveal his heart. His roots are bared. Not 'better for God', he is saying or 'better for Nineveh', but 'better for *me*'. The crux is reached. He tends to rant but God will curb his arrogance. The aftermath is not for ill but good. God's kindness wins. Not long before, he sang God's praises. 'Thou hast brought up my life from corruption, O Lord, my God.' Yes, once he had died but now he was risen. He ought to live, not shout for death. How pertinent the question, 'Doest thou well to be angry?' Its ring of reason rouses him. He knows the truth yet crudely flings his answer back. But soon the 'Not so!' complex of the Joppa quay must pass for ever. Then gratefully, his pen will fill the parchment. His book declares his 'Yes' to God. The final word is with his Master. It always is.

CHAPTER 21

THE GOOD OF THE GOURD

Meanwhile Jonah resolves to wait to the end. He will sit it out to the very last minute of the very last day. On his chosen location, east of the city, he prepares for his vigil. There is work to do ere the sun gets up. Slowly it lifts on the distant hills. The prophet pauses in the growing light. The city glistens in the dawn. Like a finger of death his long dark shadow points straight to Nineveh. Away to the south flows the Khosr and the Zab, whilst far to the west, the Tigris glitters, a brazen serpent in the sunrise. And there beyond, stretch the steppes of Jazirah, where the endless dunes lead back to Zebulun. From the west he had ventured on the wind of the Spirit. Eastwards God bore him, till Nineveh trembled, but his heart is yearning for old Gath-Hepher,[1] for its well and its winepress and his father's voice.

'As far as the east is from the west
So far hath He removed our transgressions from us.'

It was the song of the psalmist. God had done it for Israel, and had done it for Jonah. Would He do it for Gentiles? Tensely he waits for the climax of fury. How would God answer? By the east wind of judgement or the west wind of grace? O for the east wind! By that, the corn was blasted in the dream, and fruit left withered on the tree. By that, were Tyrus' oarsmen troubled and the ships of Tarshish broken. By that dread wind he was pursued till plunged into the raging deep. If from the east God's wind would

[1] Gath-Hepher means 'the winepress by the well'. Its name was expressive of Jonah's ministry, concerned as it was with 'the winepress of judgement' and 'the wells of salvation'.

blow, the overthrow of Nineveh was sure. Later it did, yet
with what irony; not for the cursing of the city but for the
curbing of the prophet. When the east wind brought the
locusts, it was the west wind that dispersed them. If the east
wind brought the drought, then the west wind brought the
rain. Did not Elijah's cloud declare its portent on a western
sea? 'When ye see a cloud rise out of the west,' said our
Lord, 'straightway, ye say, there cometh a shower, and so it
is.' Thus Jonah came. The storm clouds gathered; the skies
grew black; the thunder rolled. All seemed so ominous and
yet the threatening sky, once it had made men flee for
shelter, dispensed God's blessings on their heads. Such is
God's work as the west wind blows. The east wind kills but
the west gives life. As welcome rain, God's mercy falls.
How varied are His currents in our putrid air. His breath
is sweet. His gales sweep clean; the stormy wind, and
zephyr breeze, all keep His word.

Jonah's efforts to make himself comfortable, proved however, more strenuous than expected. For miles around
Nineveh the land had been denuded of timber. This was
due to the avid appetite of the charcoal-burners, who daily
devoured all the wood they could get. The peasantry would
walk long distances to scour the wilderness for scrub; and
go to lonely wadis where the gnarled old thickets fought in
vain with sun and sand. Sometimes a whitened tree-trunk
caught the eye, its silvery substance centuries old. The axe
would deftly hew its wood till piles of sticks stood neatly
stacked; then to the long trek back with naked feet and
weary loads. Palm fronds, perhaps, were all that Jonah
found to use. They soon would wither, yet if he waited
forty days, he must have shelter. What else would do?

The booth he made would bring back memories;
memories of leafy bowers and the feast of tabernacles. The
word employed is just the same. It held both retrospect and
prospect. Such ritual called to mind God's ceaseless care in

all their wanderings, yet looked ahead to that glad day when God's Messiah would sit enthroned. It was the 'closing festival' each year. The corn and wine were gathered in. The feast began. For labours passed, and increase gained, they thanked their God, then set their faces to the future. So will it be one day, when all their tears and toil are past. The nation brought from alien lands shall be re-born. God's Spirit shall indwell them, the covenant be realised, their frontiers assured. Then they will be the head and not the tail, and the first of the nations. They will sow a handful on the mountains. The fruit thereof will shake like Lebanon. Jerusalem shall be a joy in the earth and worshippers from every race come singing on their way to Zion. So shall millennial abundance flow; the Jew *and Gentile* shall rejoice, and there together, celebrate the feast of tabernacles. Thus God shall gather all things in and Christ shall reign. It is the final Harvest Home, for those whose forbears long ago, once lived in booths.

What Jonah thought, we do not know. He builds *his* booth and waits for harvest, but cannot see the Gentiles blessed. What of the reaping? Will it be corn, or only wine; the corn which speaks of life and blessing, or the blood-red wine that tells of judgement? The harvest in Israel embraced them both; as the psalmist says, 'Thou hast put gladness in my heart, more than in the time that their corn and wine increased.' God's harvest too, yields corn and wine. We think of the Saviour. As a corn of wheat He fell into the ground. All alone in the darkness. He died in our place. Then the first fruits came. Christ lives, and so will every saint who sleeps. How grace has blessed! But the day shall come when the grapes must be gathered. Then He who died will trample the winepress, and the wicked be purged. This two-fold harvest of our Lord, provokes to reverence. In Jonah's eyes there was no corn in Nineveh; only the vintage of his God's displeasure, only men's blood.

He felt so exhausted, for with real exertion he had scavenged. Carefully he assembled the conglomerate pieces; but even so, the shack was crude. He would have liked it bigger, better and more beautiful; something more permanent. No sooner did he sit in it, than he wanted to improve it. Had he been preaching, he would never have coped. But now he had leisure; nor did he feel guilty. His 'bit' had been done. He was free to relax. And the booth, you could say, was still part of the work. The thing was so reasonable, and even advisable; a kind of necessity and hardly a luxury. Although not preaching, he was of course still much involved. The booth was important as an instrument of survey. He needed it to assess results. He must discern the outcome of his mission and this was his vantage point. So whether the retreat be viewed as serving himself, or serving the work, it really made no difference, for he and the work were inseparable. What served him and kept him fit, *was* of service to the work. No-one would ever know how he had preached and travelled and toiled and suffered. He had been totally expended. There is a limit to what one man can do, or even should do. You have to stop sometimes and take stock of things, whatever people say. Anyway the younger prophets were developing now. Amos and Hosea had started to preach and that was something. Who could tell? This might even be his last major mission. He surely felt like a forty-day break. That one day in Nineveh! He would never forget it! Once all was over he would make tracks for home . . . Ah, how we deceive ourselves, who try to excuse ourselves!

Jonah was so weakened in getting his booth together, that he could not have preached anyway. In fact, he was so ill-humoured by the time he was finished that he had neither strength nor desire to enjoy it. The man who seeks for souls receives authority from heaven, but he who seeks for status wants security on earth. Such hopes are vain. The heights of human glory are always chill and lonely. No wonder Jonah found no peace.

The trouble with his booth was this. It was just a man-made monstrosity, composed of sticks and garbage. It was conceived and constructed by a carnal mind acting independently of God. It was not born out of the mind of God and the life of the Spirit, but out of the mind and spirit of Jonah. Just as he had found a ship going to Tarshish and enough silver to pay the fare, so now he had found enough dead wood and Ninevite refuse to make him a booth. 'The Lord is Thy shade,' sang the psalmist, thus the booth was an insult. No wonder the Lord of the harvest ignored it. If leisure and pleasure, hobbies and home, diversion and relaxation are merely the products of a tired mind craving for a break, then they hold nothing for God. These things must be equally the product of spiritual exercise as are our efforts in public service. What I am and do at leisure must be born of the Spirit, just as much, as what I am and do in labour. There is no moment when God leaves us to our own devices. The man of God has no spare time, no extra cash, no surplus energy. All time, resources, strength and powers are gifts of God. They are the content, of a work and rest, His choice ordains. There is no frontier of 'His' or 'ours'. *He* is the author of refreshment. The One who sends the reapers out, is He who calls the reapers in. Both acts are His. When Jesus wields the initiative, then rest is rest indeed, not some imagined right I try to sneak, when God is otherwise engaged. We never need to rob our Saviour, or pilfer what our Master owns. The hands that fed the multitude, still held in store a basket each, for those who served. He does not ask two hundred pence. The bread was His. He gave it from His Father's bounty, for:

'Back of the loaf is the snowy flour
And back of the flour, the mill.

K

And back of the mill are the wheat and shower
And the sun and the Father's will.'[2]

True rest and sustenance for saints, grows out of Christ. It
is not found in lifeless things. They will infect us. All food
and raiment, shade and shelter come from Jesus.

So grows the gourd. How swiftly He provides. This is
God's work not man's. Born out of life, it yields a living
shade. It draws its strength from hidden springs. It bur-
geons upward in His power, and He alone appoints its
function. God does not pander to our asking, nor does he
ever entertain. His ordered respite has its meaning. Ease is
no end. It too must serve. The gourd's intent is clearly
stated. It made a shadow for his head. How vulnerable the
labourer's mind.

Both in the deep and in the desert, Jonah's head received
attention. The Lord discerns the puckered brow. He did
God's work without God's thinking. The cursèd weeds still
twirled his reason. Although God gives this brief relief, His
heat will scorch those tendrils soon. How God remembers!
He knows our measure. This gift is sent to save from 'grief',
though only here, this word is so translated. In almost every
other place, it reads as 'wickedness'. The word, we note, has
been used earlier. It is the 'wickedness' of Nineveh.[3] Sin is
the same wherever found, whether in root or fruit, in saint
or sinner. A grief to us, it is of greater grief to God. He
will not have it in his own. Divine refreshment would
revive that mind exposed to Satan's wiles, through tears
and tension. Instruction and correction must go on. God
will not cease, till what He authors is complete. The gourd
is good, though not for ever. The God who made it is our
portion. He only is our all in all. He gives and takes away,
that He, Himself, might be our bliss.

[2] Dr Babcock.
[3] Jonah 1 v. 2.

CHAPTER 22

THE DAY OF THE WORM

Everything was wonderful! Who could have imagined a plant coming out of the ground like that? It was simply magnificent, and still it grew higher. The cool refreshing shade of its luxuriant leaves filled Jonah with delight. He was almost childish in his reaction. It quite transformed him. For the moment he completely forgot about dying and began to relax. Now and again he still scanned the city, for should anything happen, he would be sorry to miss it. To what degree he traced the gourd to its Creator, it is difficult to say. 'He was glad for the gourd' we are told, but hardly glad in his Lord? Still, it was the Lord God who had prepared it, and he as a child of the covenant had been blessed by it. The title of deity is clearly significant. God here is the Lord God, and He was *that* to Israel. The gourd therefore depicts those blessings the believer enjoys by reason of his special relationship. Although the gourd was a natural species known to the Hebrews as 'qiqayon' and to botanists, today, as 'palma christi', its appearance and growth were no doubt miraculous. The Lord God had acted for one of His own by taking something natural and speaking through it supernaturally. God's creation is always telling of His Godhead, but when, as Lord, He specially meets His people's need, how very closely they should listen. Such education is most personal. To think that for this particular servant, in one particular place, He would grow one particular gourd, demands reflection. It is our business, not just to be delighted, but to stand in awe; to kneel in wondering thankfulness and seek the moral good His gift intends. Even whilst he built his booth, the gourd was growing. Impetuously he strove for comfort, quite unaware a plan of care was well in hand. 'Your Father knoweth . . .' Jesus said. Had Jonah sought his Master's face he might have learned his Master's secret. Quickly surprised, he is easily shattered; his faith is brittle. See how it breaks! Yes, the whole thing was extraordinary! It had been demanding, working in the heat, but now the gourd had come along, the prospect seemed at once more pleasant. Helped by a good night's rest, he awoke the next morning feeling quite different. He was going to enjoy these days after all. As the first glint of sunrise flecked the dunes with gold, he began to bestir himself. His first thought was for the gourd. Why if it went on growing like it did yesterday, it would be like a cedar tomorrow! As he lay wrapped in his mantle, and peering up through the foliage, he gradually grew conscious of patches of sky. Soon they sparkled like stars in the lush green canopy and all around him the bright warm sunshine came pouring through. It was time to get up! The sand was still cool to his feet, as he surveyed the massive plant. Then he looked a little closer. He could hardly believe it. He felt sure it was drooping. The sense of luxuriant growth was gone. As the sun beat down, its maze of branches began to subside. The fresh green shoots curled back and the whole vast structure sagged to the ground. The hours passed and there it lay, brown as the dust from which it grew. The effect on Jonah was devastating. Who was responsible? We see him digging in the sand, until he holds the rotting root. The man is furious. His smouldering anger flames again. He finds a single coccus worm – a 'toleah', as the Hebrews called it. How happily it wriggles, so full and fat from hours of feasting. He could have cursed it! His mood is moulded by misfortune. He is not mellowed by God's mercy. He lets his changing lot control him. Allergic to his circumstances, his 'self' convulses. Alive to

God, he should have praised him, but now his see-saw feelings fool him. One moment up – 'I've got a gourd!' One moment down – 'A worm has caught me!' He loses grip. Joyous when prosperous, he grows bitter when battered. He shows his symptoms. What trifling things will put the soul-sick man on edge.

Jonah, though slow to acknowledge the blessing of the gourd, is quick to pin its blight on God. The man is a mirror. His mood reflects us. Begrudging thanks, we haste to blame. For years we taste His daily goodness, yet should He chasten, we discount Him. The *Lord God* made the gourd but note again the change of title. *God* made the worm. We see Him, then, in either role. As 'Lord and God', He is Covenant-Keeper: as simply 'God', the Great Creator. Because we are His covenant-children, we know His special blessings! But even so, the creature's suffering does not pass us by. As saved of the Lord, we taste redemption's fruit, but as still in the body, the sorrows of humanity must frequently be ours. Covenant blessing does not exempt, as yet, from nature's trials. As Paul records, 'Not only they, but ourselves also, who have the firstfruits of the Spirit, even we ourselves groan within ourselves, waiting for the adoption, to wit the redemption of our body.' We have received good from the hands of the Lord, but as members of a fallen race, shall we not receive 'evil'? This is inescapable, however undesirable. We must not resent having a gourd today, and a worm tomorrow, but dare to believe that 'all things work together for good to them that love God, to them who are the called according to His purpose'. We may be puzzled, but His goal is sure. This is the 'good' He has in view to bring us to the image of His Son. Not only must we learn contentment but have discernment. 'I am instructed,' says Paul (and the word means 'initiated'). 'both to be full and to be hungry, both to abound and suffer need.' No wonder he could rejoice in

the Lord always, then shout again, 'Rejoice!' He grasped
the lesson of the worm. The whale declares God's judgement, the worm His discipline. The Cross and its meaning
we admit at conversion. It is practice in crisis that shows
forth the Crucified. Some thank the Lord for gourds. God
must be thanked for worms. He brings His blessing
through them both. His love refreshes, though it reduces.
Spiritual relief and moral renewal go hand in hand, else
were the gift our rest, and not the Giver. The man who joys
in his Redeemer, still has his song:

> 'The Lord gave
> And the Lord hath taken away.
> Blessed be the Name of the Lord.'

Jonah is now defenceless. His booth has proved useless
and the gourd short-lived. He is back to square one,
nursing his grievance in the morning light. Having tasted
the living shelter of his Lord's provision, his own poor
shack no longer draws him. Our fabrications never equal
God's creations. Once rest beneath His shadow, and all our
works will fade and pall. The air grows hotter as the sun
climbs high. But Jonah waits. He will not move till God
has acted. A scorching breath strikes at his face. A wind
arises. He sees the grains of sand go eddying by. The far
horizon clouds with dust and soon long angry swathes
streak out beyond the groves of cacti. They look like ser-
pents on the move. The hiss and whisper of the sands is
ominous. And yet the sun shines on, a molten ball of brass,
whose sullen heat fills all the desert floor with fire. The east
wind of destruction blows. Its course is set; westward to
Nineveh. Is this the hour?

His head is burning like a furnace. A fearful dehydra-
tion grips him. His vision blurs. Once more his will to live
declines and soon the whimpering words return. 'It is
better for me,' he groans, 'to die than to live.' The withered

leaves lie almost buried in the shifting sands. He grows aggressive. 'Doest thou well to be angry,' says God, 'for the gourd?' He is vexed for the plant, yet unmoved for the people. His dry parched throat croaks out the answer. 'I do well to be angry,' he says, 'even to death.' His attitude seems quite incurable, yet strange to say, God's healing is not far away.

Notice how Jonah's 'head' recurs once more. This is the third time in the story. His sickness centres in the mind. His thoughts confound him. First, as we noted, the weeds wrapped round it, for his was a 'corrupt mind'. Devoured in the depths, God dealt with its enmity, for his was a 'carnal mind'. Then by the gourd it was carefully shaded for his was a tired mind. But Jonah reverts and God turns the heat on. He will burn out the curse, and create a 'renewed mind'. 'So the sun beat on the head of Jonah, that he fainted.' 'Consider Jesus,' says the Hebrew writer in later years, 'lest ye be weary and faint in your minds.' But Jonah will consider nothing. Like his ancestors in the wilderness, hungry and thirsty, his soul faints within him. Yet all he feels is spoken now. The evil of his natural-man comes out in full. His sin abounds; but God pursues till grace succeeds. Though overwhelmed with flaming passion, his Lord *will* have him. His loving heart is opened to him, and as He speaks, we sense this whispering lament:

Long years ago, Jonah *I* too, had a gourd,
when the earth was still young
and the world was a wilderness.
There in the desert, I planted a garden,
not far from this place
where you first built your booth.
It became an oasis of verdure and order,
a bridgehead of peace in the midst of the chaos,
a place where I walked in the cool of the day.

And the gourd that I planted was tended and vibrant;
a source of refreshment, of pleasure and joy.

But a worm came and struck it
and caused it to wither;
My gourd, even Adam,
who fell to the ground.
Yet not with surprise did I see all this happen,
for I made the worm, Jonah – fashioned its beauty
made it to serve Me, in treason and duty.
    All this is a mystery still hidden in history;
    nor can it be known on this side of My Throne.

Then I looked on My man, who had faded as petals;
and I yearned for My gourd, whose flesh was as grass.
I said, I will spare him, will save and revive him,
this creature so mortal that died in a night.
So I came to deliver My man who had withered.
By truth I exposed him.
Through death, I reclothed him.
I promised a seed and a means of restoring,
Till the worm was dismayed
and the devil went roaring.
    For man was My image! Yes, man was My glory!
    O should I not spare? You must think on My story.

And now in the city, I see Adam's children
all withered and worn by the work of the worm.
I see the young infants and very much cattle.
They do not suspect Me.
My love shall direct Me.
    Why should the worm conquer, when I am Creator?
    My gourd was so fair. Then should I not spare?

Just think how you felt, Jonah –
Your gourd and its coolness!
How happy you were in the heat of the day!

You took it and used it,
whose hands had not made it.
You never imagined a worm would invade it;
but then when it happened, you went all to pieces.
You shouted me down with your crude exegesis.
How could such a gourd be struck down in a night?
The thing was outrageous! You wanted to fight!
   Yet its life was not yours, though you claimed its
      refreshment,
    who flared up in anger and swore at its blight!

O give Me your answer, out there in the sunshine.
Come purge out defiance and grow to your God.
O learn to love people, regardless of background.
Don't weep for a gourd, or shed tears for a pod!

Just one thing more, Jonah, I need now to tell you,
a thing not quite realised away there in Israel;
That you were a gourd to me, you were my treasure.
Your faith in that desert, afforded Me pleasure.
So I called you and taught you and made you My vessel.
I sent you to Nineveh, the good to the evil;
To thunder My judgements, to warn and to shade them;
To call to repentance, to seek and upbraid them
   They heard and believed Me. They truly received Me
   So grace pardoned all, for they answered My call.

But a worm at your roots, cut you off from My favour.
Your green leaf turned brown, you were left without
   savour.
O you raged and you pouted.
You withered with madness.
Twas I whom you flouted
and Mine is the sadness
as meanly you stand and meanly you stare.
Have you never had children? How can you not care?

O don't be a worm, Jonah! Don't gnaw at My purpose!
O don't play the maggot at the root of My plans!
For though I have made you, and sent you, and used you
I too can destroy you, as well as employ you.
    Yet *still* I have pity on you and the city.
    O rest in My care! — *I* have chosen to spare.

EPILOGUE

Now shall we be personal?

It was during my first week in Shanghai that it happened, whilst walking with an aged missionary through the crowded streets. Suddenly on the pavement, I spotted a little bundle of rags. 'What's that?' I asked. 'That,' he said, 'is a baby someone's thrown away. There's a truck that goes round and collects them up . . .' Somehow we did not stop but went on down the streets just walking and talking. I had things to attend to in the port of Shanghai, things like my baggage and the cashing of cheques . . .

Almost a year later, I was staying at a Chengtu mission hostel, in China's far west. Each day as I walked through the compound gates, I noticed a young lad lying there on the ground. He had so many sores. A week went by and the rebuke of God entered my conscience. I approached a Chinese Christian and together we returned to the quiet enclosure. I was deeply disturbed. For a moment I looked at the vacant footwalk, that desolate spot where the boy had suffered. The child was gone. Too late for a kindness! But I had been busy, both learning the language and preaching the Truth . . .

One day in Kangting, a mountain town on the Sino-Tibetan border, I went for a walk. As I passed the Chinese barracks, I saw a coolie lying full length on the ground. Just a few yards away stood one of his fellow-countrymen, a soldier on duty. Naïvely I dismissed the situation, assuring myself that should it prove needful, the guard would assist him. A day or two later, I took the same road again, and to my horror saw that the man still lay there, dead and frozen to the earth . . . Whatever had happened? I was there for the Lord . . .

Yes, there for the Lord . . .

As indeed, was Jonah.

But now the years have passed away. Maybe the lorry came, and the babe attained to manhood. Maybe the boy found healing and works some place today. Maybe the coolie lived again . . . but no, I cannot say it . . . Each lies there, as I left him, alone and helpless on the heartless streets.

I wonder how I preached Him in that vast sad country . . .

God only knows how loveless the 'godly' man can be.

> 'Stab my soul fiercely with another's pain
> Let me walk seeing horror and stain.
> Let my hands, groping, find other hands.
> Give me a heart that divines, understands.'[1]

---

[1] The poet Teichmer.

BIBLIOGRAPHY

Aalders, G. Ch., *The Problem of the Book of Jonah*

De Haan, M. R., *Jonah: Fact or Fiction*

Fereday, W. W., *Jonah and Balaam*

Hart Davies, D. E., *Jonah: Prophet and Patriot*

Kennedy, J., *On the Book of Jonah*

Knight, G. A. F., *Ruth and Jonah*

Martin, H., *The Prophet Jonah*

Mauro, P., *The Sign of the Prophet Jonah*

Overduin, J., *The Adventures of a Deserter* (trans. from the Dutch by
    H. van Dyke)

Perowne, T. T., *Obadiah and Jonah*

Willis, G., *The Prophet Jonah*

Rescue the Perishing

Great God of Wonders

Trust & Obey